Keto Copycat Cookbook

Making the Most Popular Restaurant Dishes Ketogenic-Friendly at Home

Madison Miller

All rights reserved © 2021 by Madison Miller and The Cookbook Publisher. No part of this publication or the information in it may be quoted from or reproduced in any form by means such as printing, scanning, photocopying, or otherwise without prior written permission of the copyright holder.

This book is presented solely for motivational and informational purposes. The author and the publisher do not hold any responsibility for errors, omissions, or contrary interpretation of the subject matter herein.

The recipes provided in this book are for informational purposes only and are not intended to provide dietary advice. A medical practitioner should be consulted before making any changes in diet. Additionally, recipes' cooking times may require adjustment depending on age and quality of appliances. Readers are strongly urged to take all precautions to ensure ingredients are fully cooked to avoid the dangers of foodborne illnesses. The recipes and suggestions provided in this book are solely the opinions of the author. The author and publisher do not take any responsibility for any consequences that may result due to following the instructions provided in this book.

All the nutritional information contained in this book is provided for informational purposes only. This information is based on the specific brands, ingredients, and measurements used to make the recipe, and therefore the nutritional information is an estimate, and in no way is intended to be a guarantee of the actual nutritional value of the recipe made in the reader's home. The author and the publisher will not be responsible for any damages resulting in your reliance on the nutritional information. The best method to obtain an accurate count of the nutritional value in the recipe is to calculate the information with your specific brands, ingredients, and measurements.

ISBN 9798710605646

Printed in the United States

www.thecookbookpublisher.com

CONTENTS

INTRODUCTION	1
THE KETO DIET BASICS	3
STARTING	11
THE KETOGENIC DIET	11
SMART KETO SWAPS	21
KETO COPYCAT BREAKFAST RECIPES	29
KETO COPYCAT APPETIZERS AND SNACKS RECIPES	57
KETO COPYCAT SALAD AND SOUP RECIPES	77
KETO COPYCAT CHICKEN RECIPES	97
KETO COPYCAT BEEF AND PORK RECIPES	119
KETO COPYCAT FISH SEAFOOD RECIPES	139
KETO COPYCAT DESSERT RECIPES	159
RECIPE INDEX	177
APPENDIX	180

INTRODUCTION

Ever tried to make a dish from one of your favorite restaurants at home? That's exactly what copycat recipes are, recreating popular restaurant dishes at home. And if you are following the keto diet, this can be a big issue as most restaurants offer very few keto-friendly choices. But there is a solution, make favorite restaurant recipes keto-friendly! That is exactly what this cookbook is all about.

Everyone likes to dine out every once in a while—a date night with a significant other, a family dinner at a nice restaurant, lunch out or coffee with friends at a local café, or even a quick drive-by at a favorite fast food place.

There's just something about eating out that, whether alone or with company, makes eating all the more enjoyable. Maybe you think that you'll never be able to recreate the food you order at Outback Steakhouse, Starbucks, or McDonald's.

So, you go in there, wait in line for what seems like an eternity, and then pay for food that you know is way overpriced. But what if you didn't have to go through all that? What if you could be munching on a Cinnabon you made right in your own home?

No leaving the house, no waiting in line, and no spending money on expensive food—just the amazing taste of your beloved restaurant dishes and the satisfaction that you were able to recreate them all by yourself (or with friends or family). And, with the help of this cookbook, you'll be able to do just that in no time. All the recipes have been transformed into keto-friendly recipes, that are low in carbs and follow the guidelines of the ketogenic diet.

This cookbook is filled with keto copycat recipes from your favorite restaurants that you can make at home, some as quick as 30 minutes. There are over 70 recipes in this cookbook that range from breakfast meals and snacks to entrees and desserts. You'll start cooking like a restaurant keto chef in no time! But first, let get into the basics of the keto diet and what ingredients you can use to make restaurant keto-friendly meals at home.

THE KETO DIET BASICS

The keto diet is all about leading a healthy lifestyle by losing excess weight and keeping it off through defined keto ratios. If you are overweight, then you might start to think about following an effective diet plan. Or maybe your physician has recommended that you lose weight because of a chronic health condition. The keto diet is one of the top-rated diet plans to cope with obesity, kidney disease, heart disease, and many other issues.

Unlike any other diet plan, the keto diet focuses on fat intake rather than lowering fat. The keto diet is a revolutionary diet plan which burns fat rather than carbohydrates to fuel the body through the process of ketosis. This leads to improved physical health and mental stability.

The keto diet is all about low carb, high fat, and adequate protein. Most people assume that it's important to cut fats in order to lose weight. But modern research suggests that cutting sugar from the diet has a far better effect than cutting fat. Low carb diets help us to balance hormones, stabilize blood pressure, increase strength, and lose weight. And this is what the keto diet is all about.

The keto diet is an effective diet plan that is very different from other diet plans. The keto diet defines the ratio of fat, carbohydrate, and protein to consume, and this helps you stop binge eating and craving food all the time.

Let's get into the nitty-gritty of the ketogenic diet.

How Can the Keto Diet Improve My Life?

My guess is you have found yourself here, in the pages of this book, because you have become unsatisfied with a part of your life – the part that involves your health, your weight, and your energy level. Be assured, you are not alone. You stand among many who want to change how they look, and how they feel. Every one of us has followed our own path here, and have our own causes for feeling low and unhealthy.
Some of it is stress, some of it is being too busy, some of it is laziness, some of it is hereditary, and some of it might be illness, just to name a few possibilities.

But what each of us has in common is that our current state of health is, first and foremost, our own personal responsibility. Taking responsibility isn't always easy, but once you do, the most amazing thing happens: you realize you have the capability and the power to make the change. It is this realization and the desire to make that change that has brought you here, to the place where it can finally happen.

Unless you have been totally unaware of the diet industry for the past couple of decades, chances are you are familiar with low-carb diets. You have probably heard of the positive results and the supposed negative side effects. The fact is, low-carbohydrate diets are successful for the majority of people who follow them. However, the typical low-carb diet is difficult to sustain in the long term, and often people who follow the diet burn out quickly. This burnout was the reason that more and more people began looking at a new type of low-carb diet – the ketogenic diet.

The ketogenic diet shares some characteristics with a typical low-carb diet; in the initial phases you reduce your carbohydrate intake to a point where you are able to enter and maintain a state of ketosis, you don't worry about counting calories unless you want to, and you lose weight very quickly.

So, what is it that makes this plan different? A ketogenic diet is also different in a few ways. To begin with, a ketogenic diet teaches you how to eat a modest amount of carbohydrates for life, rather than in stages. Most people also feel that a ketogenic diet is less costly than the other common low-carb diets.

A ketogenic diet focuses on a higher ratio of fat. This ratio is approximately 70 percent of your calories from fat, with 20 percent coming from protein sources and about 10 percent coming from carbohydrates. Most people are a little shocked when they read that. Seventy percent from fat, are you kidding me? We are not kidding at all. This is an eating strategy that was actually developed decades ago to help reduce the occurrence and severity of seizures in epileptic children, and it has numerous health benefits.

Here is the thing – fat has received an undeserved negative reputation. First of all, you want your focus to be on healthy fats like those found in olive oil and fatty fish (which are incredibly good for your health) while limiting bad fats. Your body, including your brain, needs fat to function. Fat is a source of energy, it contains essential fatty acids, it is necessary for nerve function, it helps to maintain healthy skin, and it is absolutely essential for the transportation of fat-soluble vitamins like vitamin A, E, D, and K.

When you have this knowledge, you can begin to see how the focus on low-fat diets has actually been a detriment to our health. Protein is great, but if you eat too much of it, it can actually increase blood sugar levels temporarily, sabotaging your low-carb diet efforts. This is why the ketogenic diet is heavier in fats and less so in protein. Now that we know this, let's talk a little bit about carbohydrates.

The Good and the Bad Of Carbohydrates

In the typical diet of the western world, carbohydrates take center stage. This seems to be true whether your diet is low fat and natural or highly processed. Think for a moment about what the health and diet industry has been telling us for years. Keep it low fat, eat lots of healthy grains, and indulge in fresh fruits and vegetables. Sounds reasonable, and for the most part, it is. However, we have taken the grain aspect of it and gone too far astray. Let's say you have been trying to eat well. For breakfast you have oatmeal and fruit, lunch consists of a turkey sandwich on whole-grain bread, a snack might be some low-calorie crackers and produce and then dinner has pasta, rice, potatoes, or other starchy vegetables.

Any one of these things in a standalone category is fine. However, we bombard our bodies with an abundance of carbohydrates throughout the day, every day. Carbohydrates are not all bad. They are a source of energy for your body and can help regulate your blood sugar. Many nutritious foods that are high in carbohydrates, such as certain fruits and vegetables, are also excellent sources of fiber and valuable nutrients. The problem is the amount and quality of carbohydrates that you consume can actually damage your health, rather than heal it.

Recent studies show that it is sugar, and not necessarily fat, that is contributing to an overall increase in serious, chronic illness. Excess carbohydrates, especially those found in processed foods, contribute to an inflamed state in the body. Your body will recover from this, but then it happens again the next day and the day after that. Soon, your body loses some of its ability to recover and heal and you find yourself chronically inflamed and suffering from pain and disease.

Chronic inflammation has been shown to be a contributor to conditions such as cardiac diseases, diabetes, fibromyalgia, arthritis, inflammatory bowel disease, and even cancer. Meanwhile, we are finding that moderate amounts of healthy fats actually combat these conditions. Knowing this, we have to ask ourselves how to approach eating on a daily basis in a way that will help keep extra weight off and keep chronic illness away. There may be more than one answer to this, but the answer I would like to offer to you now is the ketogenic diet.

The ketogenic diet is formulated to supply your body with the number of fats and proteins it needs to thrive while reducing the amount of inflammation-causing carbohydrates. To begin this diet, you will limit yourself to somewhere between 20 and 60 grams of carbohydrates per day in order to enter a nutritional state known as ketosis. This is the point when your body begins using its fat stores (rather than carbohydrates) as fuel. This means that as you burn energy, you burn fat, even the stubborn fat that hasn't wanted to budge for years.

It is important to note that you will eat carbohydrates, just not as many of them, and you will become picky about the ones you consume. We will go in-depth about what foods to enjoy and which ones to avoid a little later in the book, however, what you have to look forward to is a rich and nutritious diet full of healthy fats, proteins, gorgeous green vegetables, and juicy berries, just to name a few of the delights. The ketogenic diet is healthy, weight-loss promoting, and completely satisfying.

Health Benefits Of the Ketogenic Diet

You know you will lose weight with the ketogenic diet, but your mind might be flooded with questions about how this can be good for you, so many calories, so few grains, how will this enrich my life and not just please my taste buds? The truth is, there are many ways in which the ketogenic lifestyle will benefit your health, with a reduction in weight being just the tip of the iceberg.

Here is a list of the many wonderful benefits that are within your reach when you decided to eat ketogenically.

1. You gain a healthy relationship with your appetite. It might seem that the ketogenic diet is all about overindulgence, and it is true that you might overindulge, especially during the initial weeks when you just can't believe you can have all you want of so many delicious and decadent foods. However, after the first couple of weeks, you will find that your appetite is actually suppressed, you have fewer cravings and you focus less on what your next meal or snack is going to be. If you are like so many others, you have found yourself in the position of being overweight by participating in an unhealthy relationship with food. Maybe you have become too busy to focus on nutrition and lost your focus on your health, maybe food is emotional for you, whatever has brought you here, ketosis will help you regain a balance and give you the opportunity to recognize not only when you are full, but what your body truly needs to thrive.

2. You will have improved mental clarity and focus. In the simplest terms possible, fat is good for your brain and limited carbohydrates will prevent energy crashes as your body begins to rely on the ever-present fat sources for energy. After the first week or so,

most people who eat ketogenically report having more energy and greater focus and clarity in their thinking. Some even claim they experience fewer depressive symptoms than before they started the diet.

3. Your path to a healthier lifestyle doesn't stop at the end of ketosis. Maybe you will eat ketogenically for the rest of your life, maybe you will discover that it just isn't for you. Either way, you are training your body to reset your metabolism and help you maintain a healthy weight going forward. As mentioned earlier, you will develop a healthier relationship with food, but you will also experience metabolic changes. You know about metabolism. A fast metabolism is a blessing that some people receive, while others do not. There is nothing magical about metabolism, but our bodies do metabolize food in their own way. This is part of your unique physiology that you were born with. However, just because you were born with a slow metabolism, doesn't mean you have to accept it. The ketogenic diet will help reset your metabolism so it is more efficient at burning your energy stores and helping you maintain a healthy weight.
4. It is hard to get discouraged while on the ketogenic diet. Weight comes off quickly and with little effort in the beginning. All you have to do is make the commitment.

5. You will improve your health. People who eat ketogenically have a lower occurrence of obesity, lower blood pressure, triglyceride levels, and HDL cholesterol levels.

6. You lower your risk of developing type 2 diabetes and if you are already diabetic, you can help reduce the severity of your condition. Ketogenic eating helps to relieve insulin sensitivity. Some diabetics who follow

the ketogenic diet while under a physician's supervision were able to actually remove the need for medication.

7. The list of diseases that you reduce your risk of doesn't stop at diabetes. When you adopt a ketogenic lifestyle you reduce or eliminate your risk of the following conditions:

   - heart disease
   - high blood pressure
   - stroke
   - inflammatory health conditions
   - skin ailments
   - obesity-related health conditions

This is only the beginning of the many ways your health and your life will improve with the ketogenic diet. There is so much more than what can fit within the confines of any book. Each person will have their own experience and each person will discover for themselves how empowering the ketogenic diet can be.

STARTING THE KETOGENIC DIET

The Basis of the Keto Diet, The Ketosis

Ketosis is the backbone of any low carbohydrate diet, including the ketogenic plan. Ketosis is the state your body is in when you limit the number of carbohydrates you consume, and thus force your body to use its fat stores to burn energy.

When this happens, your body releases something called ketones, which will be present in your blood and urine. The reason some people are advised to avoid low carbohydrate diets is that ketosis can be hard on people with certain health conditions, where the kidneys and liver are already compromised. In otherwise healthy people, ketosis poses no health risk.

It will take two to three days of reduced carbohydrate intake for your body to enter ketosis. You might be able to tell that this has occurred, just by an increase in urination, an almost instant reduction in weight, and other changes in how you feel. Otherwise, you can purchase something called Ketostix®, which is used to measure the number of ketones in your urine. There is an indicator that will show you when you are at peak ketone level, and where a lower maintenance level is. If you are having trouble reaching ketosis, you can reduce the number of carbohydrates you are consuming.
If you are releasing too many ketones, you can add more carbohydrates into your daily diet. You will want to stay in a peak ketosis state for the two weeks of this eating plan.

You may have heard of a dangerous condition called ketoacidosis. This is not the same thing as ketosis. It is instead a condition that is usually related to severe diabetes and can be life-threatening. If you find yourself suffering from more extreme side effects, or symptoms not listed, you should seek medical counsel to rule out the possibility of an underlying medical condition that might be contraindicated with ketosis.

The Keto Diet Guidelines

The ketogenic diet isn't actually meant to be a diet, as much as it is meant to be a dietary lifestyle. The first two weeks are a little more restrictive and require a bit more diligence; however, in the long term, the ketogenic diet is easy to maintain. I honestly dislike the idea of giving you a set of rules to follow because I know firsthand how difficult it can be to maintain a dietary mindset when you feel overburdened with a list of rules. For this reason, the list of "rules" is actually quite short. The ketogenic diet is simple in its approach, and you need to keep only a few things in mind as you set out to take charge of your life with this new way of fueling your body.

1. You Have Heard It Before but Talk to your Doctor.

Every diet or exercise plan, at least every reputable one, is going to recommend that you seek out the advice of a physician before you start. The reason this is the number one rule is not that I have to put it here, but because I honestly mean it. The ketogenic diet will work wonderfully for the majority of people. However, during the diet, you will enter a state of ketosis, which can actually cause more harm than good in people with certain health conditions.

There is a lot that happens physiologically in ketosis, and while safe for most people, your doctor should still know about your dietary lifestyle in case you encounter any health problems along the way. Besides that, it is good to have a full checkup and blood work done so you know your starting point and can see for yourself through regular checkups the improvement you are making in your life.

2. Don't Worry about the Calories.

Yes, your primary reason for wanting to eat ketogenically is probably to lose weight, but that doesn't mean you need to be in a restrictive state of mind. You do not need to worry about restricting calories for a couple of reasons. The first is that as you enter ketosis, your body burns excess fat stores and you lose water weight no matter how many calories you consume. It is possible to consume 2000, or more, calories in a day and lose weight.

You will continue to burn fat, regardless of calorie intake during the time you are in ketosis. Second, your metabolism will be reset through the process and your body will re-learn to burn fat and calories more effectively, meaning you don't have to starve yourself to lose weight. Finally, ketosis is actually an appetite suppressant. After the initial phase of the diet you will find you are hungry less often and when you do eat, you naturally desire fewer calories to feel satisfied.

So unless you have a specific reason for limiting your calories, or your doctor has recommended that you keep within a range, then don't even let calorie count cross your mind. You have far better things to spend your time thinking about.

3. Know the Ratio, but Be Flexible.

While eating ketogenically, you will limit your carbohydrates to anywhere between 20 and 60 grams per day. This is a wide range of variance because it accounts for a wider range of physiologies. I suggest starting at around 30 grams of carbohydrates per day, and adjusting up and down. For example, if you find that you enter ketosis easily at 30 grams, then you may want to try adding carbohydrates five grams at a time to determine your limit.

If you are having trouble entering ketosis at 30 grams, then you might want to decrease your intake by five grams until you reach your ketosis threshold. It is not recommended that you go below 20 grams of carbohydrates per day. The general ratio for the ketogenic diet is 70-20-10. This means you should get 70 percent of your calories from fats, 20 percent of your calories from protein, and 10 percent from carbohydrates. Do not get obsessive about this. If you end up at 65-25-10 or 70-22-8 or anything close, it is fine. Just keep the majority of your calories from fat and keep your grams of carbohydrates in check.

4. Move a Little.

This ketogenic diet doesn't come with an exercise program, however, a little dedication to daily movement is a good thing. First of all, you do not need to exercise in order to lose weight while on the ketogenic diet, but it will help boost your results.

Secondly, if you eat ketogenically for a long period of time, you will need to do a little weight resistance training to help keep your muscles strong and not lose any muscle mass and finally, some of the foods on the approved list, combined with limited carbohydrate and fiber intake, can lead to constipation. Daily exercise can help keep your bowels working properly.

5. Keep Hydrated.

This is true whether you are on a diet or not, but during ketosis, you are going to be losing water weight as well as fat. This means you have to take extra care to replenish your body with fluids throughout the day. Adequate water intake will also prevent some of the potential side effects of ketosis.

6. Keep an Open Mind.

When you start any diet there will be highs and lows. Days when you are excited and enthused and days when you just want to cave in. the ketogenic diet has the advantage of offering you as much to eat as you want and encourages you to stay satisfied, however, there will be days when you really just want a big piece of cake or a slice of pizza.

When this happens, think of what you can do and have, rather than what you can't. For example, if you are craving pizza why not make yourself a snack stacker with all of the pizza ingredients, except the crust. Even heat it up to make the cheese nice and melty. You might not be able to indulge in cake, but what about a bar of chocolate, peanut butter, and coconut milkshake? Do not deprive yourself, but be open to the many ketogenic possibilities.

Calculating Percentages

As mentioned before, your ketogenic daily diet does not need to strictly adhere to the 70 fat/20 protein/10 carb rule, but it does need to be close. Most of the time this can be achieved just through being observant and aware of what you eat. However, you might like more of a feeling of control and structure. For that reason, I am including a brief explanation of how to calculate percentages.

If you want to take a look at the food you are about to eat or have already eaten, and figure out the percentage of calories from fat, protein, and carbohydrates, you need to know the following numbers:

- 1 gram of fat has 9 calories
- 1 gram of protein has 4 calories
- 1 gram of carbohydrate has 4 calories

As you can see, gram for gram fat has more than twice the caloric count of protein and carbohydrates.

If you eat something with 500 total calories, you might see a breakdown like this:

- 38 g of fat
- 27.5 g of protein
- 12 g of carbohydrates

Each gram of fat has 9 calories, so 38 g x 9 calories = 342 fat calories
Each gram of protein has 4 calories, so 27.5 g x 4 calories = 110 protein calories
Each gram of carbohydrates has 4 calories, so 12 g x 4 calories = 48 carbohydrate calories.

We end up with a calorie total of 500, broken down into 342/110/48

To calculate percentages, we divide the calorie category by the total number of calories:

- 342 calories/500 calories x 100 = 68% fat calories
- 110 calories/500 calories x 100 = 22% protein calories

These ratios are not exact to 70 and 20, but they are close and they leave the remaining carbohydrate calories at approximately 10%.

The widely acceptable percentages to follow a ketogenic diet are:

- **60–75% of calories from fat**
- **10% of calories from carbs**
- **15–30% of calories from protein**

You can also use this formula to set a specific number of calories you plan to consume and break down how many fats, protein, and carbohydrate grams you will need. For example:

2,000 daily calories

- 70% of 2000 = 1400 fat calories
- 20% of 2000 = 400 protein calories
- 10% of 2000 = 200 carbohydrate calories

Now we take the information about calories per gram from above to figure out how many grams of each you need.

- 1400 fat calories / 9 calories per gram = 155.5 g of fat
- 400 protein calories / 4 calories per gram = 100 g of protein
- 200 carbohydrate calories / 4 calories per gram = 50 g of carbohydrate

These calculations are simple once you get used to them, however, remember that you do not need to do these calculations on the ketogenic diet. These instructions are only here in case you choose to do so.

Foods to Have and Foods to Avoid

Here is the section you have been looking for; what exactly can you eat while on the ketogenic eating plan? This diet is actually quite intuitive if you just remember to focus on healthy fats and steer away from carbohydrates. Fruit is limited to berries in this initial portion of the diet, after that, small amounts of other fruits can be added.

Vegetable consumption is encouraged as long as you avoid starchy vegetables such as potatoes, corn, carrots, and yams. Green is best when it comes to ketogenic vegetables. To make your meal planning and shopping simpler, here is a list of some of the best ketogenic foods and the biggest ones to avoid.

Yes foods

- Heart-healthy, fatty fish such as salmon, tuna, and trout
- Most meats, including some with higher fat content. Just remember that you can eat any meat you want, but keep healthy proteins in your diet and not just super fatty ones.
- Heart-healthy oils such as coconut oil, olive oil, and avocado oil
- Avocados
- Olives
- Eggs
- Butter
- Heavy cream (preferable to milk which has a higher carbohydrate content)

- Full fat sour cream, cream cheese, crème fraiche, cottage cheese, and other cheeses
- Unsweetened coconut milk and almond or other kinds of nut-based milk
- Low carbohydrate vegetables such as spinach, kale, leek, fennel, broccoli, salad greens, and tomatoes. Stay away from starchy and sweet vegetables.
- Strawberries, blueberries, raspberries, and blackberries in small portions
- Walnuts, almonds, and other nuts
- Chia and flax seeds
- Herbs and most spices
- Unsweetened beverages including some caffeine
- Lots of water

Foods to avoid

- Grains, including bread, pasta, rice, and cereals
- Fruits, except for the noted berries
- Beans and legumes
- Starchy vegetables
- Low-fat dairy products
- Sweetened dairy products
- Sweetened beverages
- Alcohol
- Processed foods
- Baked goods, candies, and other sweets
- Unhealthy cooking oils

Initial Side Effects and Precautions

If you have ever been on a diet before, then you know there are almost always some minor side effects as your body adjusts and accepts your new style of eating. Some common side effects, which almost always fade after the first week, include:

- Headaches
- Fatigue
- Sleep disturbances
- Frequent urination
- Lightheadedness
- Constipation
- Muscle cramps

These symptoms are mostly proof that your body is entering and adjusting to ketosis. There are a couple of things you can do to reduce or eliminate these effects. Most importantly, keep yourself hydrated; secondly, make sure you are taking in enough sodium. As you enter ketosis, your body will eliminate excess sodium so you might have to compensate. You might also want to consider a solid nutritional supplement, and if your symptoms are severe try adding an extra five grams of carbohydrates per day until your symptoms lessen.

Some people should not restrict the number of carbohydrate calories they consume for medical reasons. Please consult a physician before going on the keto diet, especially if you have any of the following health conditions.

- Diabetes
- Liver disease
- Kidney disease
- Pancreatic disease
- Gall bladder disease
- Gastric bypass surgery
- Poor nutritional status

- Pregnancy
- Lactation

Any chronic condition should be addressed before beginning this diet.

SMART KETO SWAPS

Comfort foods are truly comforting and magical, and when you can prepare them with low-carb, high-fat Keto rule – they are ultimate magic. With few smart keto-friendly swaps, you can convert any regular pantry into a keto-friendly pantry.

Keto-Friendly Healthy Fats

When it comes to cooking fats, you do not need much of a swaps. When you are consuming keto comfort foods in your routine meals, your recipes need lots of healthy cooking fats to enable your body to burn them as a fuel source. The question if how to separate unhealthy fats from healthy fats. Saturated fatty acids, also known as SFAs, are consider a valuable source of healthy fats such as ghee, butter, coconut oil, olive oil, MCT oil, lard, and tallow. These healthy fats are anti-inflammatory and stable; they prevent oxidation and improve holistic health.
Butter, ghee, cheddar cheese, heavy cream, sour cream, cream cheese and crème fraiche are high with SFAs, and that is why they are used frequently in keto comfort foods.

Unhealthy Fats

When on a Ketogenic diet, fat sources that are high with polyunsaturated fatty acids (PUFAs) and trans-fats must be avoided. They are source of unhealthy, bad fats that leads to body inflammation. They also put you at higher risk of developing heart diseases.
Avoid unhealthy fat sources that are high with PUFAs such as vegetable shortening, margarine, partially hydrogenated oils, and hydrogenated oils. Always check nutritional labels to confirm that your cooking fat does not have any of these sneaky bad fats.

Natural Sweeteners

Natural sweeteners are best Keto swaps for regular table sugar. Maple syrup, honey, high fructose corn syrup, and agave must be avoided too as they increase carbohydrate values of any recipe and moreover, they also increase blood sugar levels. Apart from causing inflammation, they also put you off ketosis.

Replace table sugar, honey, high fructose corn syrup, maple syrup and agave with any of the following natural sweetener options.

Swerve

Swerve is a popular sweetener that is zero-calorie sweetener showing no effect on blood sugar levels. Swerve is easy to swap with 1:1 ratio of table sugar. Just replace equal amount of Swerve with sugar quantity mentioned in a particular recipe.

Erythritol

Produced through natural fermentation in fruits, erythritol is another zero calorie sugar substitute that is more popularly available in market in granular form. Erythritol is a sugar alcohol and used quite frequently in all types of Keto recipes. It is available in both granular and powdered form. If you are using granular erythritol, it is also recommended that you crush into a powder form for ease of use.

When using erythritol, recipe mixture might become dry. In order to create liquid balance, you can add more stevia drops or simply water until you get desired pre-baking consistency.

Monk Fruit

Monk fruit is a natural sweetener sourced from a plant. Just like erythritol, monk fruit is too a zero calorie sweetener that can be used as a sugar substitute. It is available in both granular and liquid form with granular being a popular choice of use.

Stevia Granular and Stevia Liquid

Stevia a quite popular plant-based sweetener that is available in both varieties of stevia liquid drops and stevia granular. You can replace one with another in each recipes. Conversion chart for stevia granular to stevia drops and vice versa comes with the pack.

Stevia Glycerite

Available in thick liquid form, stevia glycerite has similar consistency of honey. It is a different form of sweetener than stevia liquid drops. Do not confuse stevia liquid drops with stevia glycerite. It offers less bitter aftertaste than stevia granular or stevia drops, and that is why many people prefer to use glycerite instead of granular or drops.

Yacon Syrup

Sourced from Yacon roots, this thick syrup tastes like molasses. It contains fructose and relatively expensive than other most natural sweeteners mentioned above.

Natural Sweetener Usage and Conversion

Swerve is a popular choice amongst natural keto-friendly sweetener options for keto comfort food recipes. As mentioned earlier, it is simple 1:1 swap with your table sugar. However, if you prefer to use other natural sweetener than Swerve; following are your conversion options.

1 cup sugar = 1 cup Swerve = 1 1/3 cup powdered erythritol
1 cup sugar = 1 cup Swerve = 1 cup powdered erythritol + 1 teaspoon stevia glycerite
1 cup sugar = 1 cup Swerve = 1 tablespoon stevia glycerite
1 cup sugar = 1 cup Swerve = Liquid stevia (a few drops)
1 cup sugar = 1 cup Swerve = Monk fruit liquid (a few drops)
1 cup sugar = 1 cup Swerve = 1 cup monk fruit granular/powdered
1 cup sugar = 1 cup Swerve = 2 cups Yacon syrup

Other Keto-Friendly Swaps

Many of your routine foods are high with carbohydrates and sugar. However, the good news is that there are numerous keto friendly substitutions that help you to easily convert routine comfort food recipes into a keto comfort food.

Wheat Flour and All Purpose Flour

Many desserts, soups, breakfast, pizza, pasta and main course recipes call for the use of wheat flour or all-purpose flour. However, these flours are not suitable to use for keto comfort foods as in tremendously increases carbohydrate values. Coconut and almond flours are the most popular keto swaps that you can replace in 1:1 ratio with wheat flour or all-purpose flour.

Made from blanched ground almonds, almond flour is rich with healthy fats and more importantly, it is low in carbohydrates. Coconut flour is yet another popular keto swap. If you prefer coconut-based taste in your comfort foods than nutty flavor, you can easily swap coconut flour with almond flour in same 1:1 ratio.

Made from ground dried coconut meat, recipes made from coconut flour are fluffy in texture and with moist consistency. It is a rich source of fibers as well as healthy fats, and is low in carbohydrates too.

Breadcrumbs in recipes can also be replaced by coconut flour or almond flour.

Pasta and Spaghetti

Zucchini noodles or Zoodles is the most common swap for regular pasta or whole wheat pasta. You can made them using a spiralizer.

Other swap options are Japanese shirataki noodles, or spiralized Spaghetti squash. Made from konjac plant, Japanese shirataki noodles contain zero carb and loaded with fibers.

Substitute 1 cup whole wheat pasta with 10 cups zucchini noodles or 10 cups cabbage pasta or noodles prepared from 6 stalks broccoli.

Lasagna Noodles

Your favorite lasagna noodles can be substituted for zucchini slices (thick cut) or sliced eggplant.

Rice and Quinoa

Substitute ½ cup uncooked quinoa or 2/3 cup uncooked white rice with 4 cups cauliflower rice.

Potatoes and Sweet Potatoes

Substitute 1 cup diced potatoes or ¾ cup diced sweet potatoes with 4 cups mashed cauliflower.

For hash browns, you can substitute with spaghetti squash or chopped cauliflower florets.

French Fries, Potato Chips or Potato Cubes

Our all-time favourite French Fries can be substituted with baked carrot sticks, zucchini fries, turnip fries, green bean fries or daikon fries.

Replace potato or sweet potato cubes with bite-sized cubes made from zucchini, green beans or carrots. Peel the vegetables first before cutting into cubes.

Substitute potato chips with healthy kale chips or green bean fries. Another healthy fat rich substitutes are American cheese crisps and Parmesan cheese crisps. For American cheese, cut into squares of 1X1-inch and microwave until crisps by placing them over a parchment paper. For parmesan cheese, shave it and add it in a frying pan. Heat pan until cheese is chewy and melts completely.

Beans

Beans (black beans, kidney beans, chickpeas, pinto beans etc.) are healthy ingredients for any recipe, they are rich with minerals, vitamins and protein. However, they also contain some carbohydrates that increase carb values in keto recipes. Green beans are still acceptable for keto recipes as it contains fewer carbs as compared to other bean varieties. The same also applies for lentils.

Replace beans in recipes with diced eggplant, cooked mushrooms, or boiled peanuts in 1:1 ratio.

Milk

Regular dairy milk is high with lactose. When we consume lactose, it gets broken down into simple sugar form in intestines. 1 cup of whole milk contains around 11 grams of carbohydrates.

Best milk substitutes (dairy and non-dairy) for keto friendly swaps are unsweetened coconut milk, unsweetened almond milk, unsweetened cashew milk, unsweetened soy milk, dairy half and half cream, heavy whipping cream, or heavy cream.

In order to replace milk with keto-friendly milk substitute, you simply follow 1:1 ratio. If a recipe calls for 2 tablespoon whole milk or regular milk, just replace it with 2 tablespoon of your choice of keto friendly milk substitute.

Buttermilk

When a recipe calls for the use of buttermilk, you can substitute it with sour cream mixed with water. Sour cream has that tangy flavor as it is prepared through fermentation process using lactic acid bacteria. It has thicker consistency than milk and that is why it is needed to be diluted using water to match with milk consistency.

Substitute 1 cup of butter milk with ¾ cup of sour cream and ¼ cup water. Combine sour cream and water in a mixing bowl; whisk to combine well. Use in recipe as directed.

Fruits

Most fruits are high with carbs and cannot be used for keto comfort recipes, if a recipe call for the use of any fruit. Replace them with keto friendly fruits such as blueberries, raspberries, strawberries and cantaloupe. However, these fruits are allowed in moderation when you are on a Ketogenic diet plan. Another option is to completely remove fruit from recipe and try making it without any fruits.

Crackers

Replace them with Parmesan cheese crisps, flax crackers, carrot crisps, cucumber crisps, zucchini crisps and celery crisps.

Corn Kernels – Cornmeal - Corn Flour

Corn kernels are high with carbohydrates and that is why it avoided in most Keto recipes. Corn in recipes can be substituted with keto friendly vegetable such as cauliflower florets, artichokes, asparagus, broccoli florets, and Brussels sprouts. al
Made from corn, both corn meal and corn flour is also avoided when following a keto diet. Simple substitute for both is superfine almond flour.

Baking Soda and Baking Powder

Many people wonder if they can freely use baking soda and baking powder for baking without increasing carbohydrate values. The good news is that baking soda does not contain any carbs and it can be freely used for all types of Keto comfort food recipes. Baking powder does contain carb but that is quite less; per teaspoon of baking powder contains a minimal carbohydrate value of 1.3 grams.

Flaxseed Meal

Flaxseed meal is also known as linseed. Just like coconut and almond flour, it is low in carbohydrates, and rich with fiber as well as omega-3 fatty acids. It is rarely used as a standalone flour. It is used in addition to almond or coconut flour for preparing cookies, muffins, breads etc. for variety of texture and improve nutritional density.

Psyllium Husk Powder

Less commonly used in Keto recipes. Psyllium husk powder is more frequently used in Keto bread recipes as a binding agent than other types of baking recipes. This low-carb, high-fiber, high-fat powder makes an ideal replacement for xanthan gum and also eggs (if you prefer egg-less baking). However, try to minimize its consumption, if you have a sensitive digestive system as it is also used as a laxative agent.

Now that we have all the information, let get started with the delicious keto copycat recipes!

KETO COPYCAT BREAKFAST RECIPES

Pink Drink (Starbucks)

A super easy-to-make cold dessert type drink that is super delicious too. This yummy drink is packed with heavy cream and sugar-free vanilla syrup.

Serves 1 | Prep time 10 minutes

Ingredients
1 strawberry tea bag
1 raspberry tea bag
1 cup boiling water
2 tablespoons erythritol

1½ cups ice water
¼ cup full-fat coconut milk
3 fresh strawberries
Pinch of xanthan gum

Directions
1. Place the tea bags in a mug and pour the boiling water over them.
2. Cover and steep for 5 minutes.
3. Add the erythritol and stir until completely dissolved.
4. Add ice water and stir.
5. In a blender, pulse the tea mixture, coconut milk, strawberries, and xanthan gum until smooth.
6. Serve chilled.

Nutrition (per serving)
Calories 133, fat 12.1 g, carbs 5.2 g, sugar 2.8 g,
Protein 1.2 g, sodium 31 mg

Pumpkin Spice Frappuccino (Starbucks)

A fall-time favorite breakfast drink. Pumpkin is blended with coffee, almond milk, coconut milk, and pumpkin pie spice.

Serves 2 | Prep time 10 minutes

Ingredients
⅔ cup canned pure pumpkin
4 teaspoons instant coffee granules
1 tablespoon erythritol
1 teaspoon vanilla extract
1½ teaspoon pumpkin pie spice plus extra for sprinkling
⅔ cup unsweetened coconut milk
⅔ cup unsweetened almond milk
2 cups ice cubes
2 tablespoons whipped cream

Directions
1. Add all of the ingredients except for the whipped cream to a high-power blender and pulse until smooth.
2. Pour into 2 serving glasses and top with whipped cream.
3. Sprinkle with extra pumpkin pie spice.

Nutrition (per serving)
Calories 110, fat 7.5 g, carbs 9 g, sugar 3.1 g,
Protein 1.6 g, sodium 70 mg

Ham and Cheese Omelet (Denny's)

A scrumptious omelet for your breakfast table. This ham, eggs and cheese-loaded omelet is delicious as well.

Serves 1 | Prep time 10 minutes | Cooking time 5 minutes

Ingredients
3 eggs
3 tablespoons water
⅛ teaspoon salt
⅛ teaspoon pepper
1 tablespoon butter
½ cup fully-cooked ham, cubed
¼ cup Swiss cheese, shredded

Directions
1. In a bowl, beat the eggs with water, salt, and pepper.
2. In a small nonstick skillet, melt the butter over medium-high heat.
3. Add the egg mixture and cook for 1–2 minutes or until set.
4. Push the cooked edges toward the center, letting the uncooked portion flow underneath.
5. Place the ham on one side of the egg mixture and sprinkle with cheese.
6. Fold the other side over the filling and transfer the omelet to a plate.
7. Serve hot.

Nutrition (per serving)
Calories 504, fat 38 g, carbs 5 g, sugar 1.4 g,
Protein 35.2 g, sodium 900 mg

Colorado Omelet (IHOP)

A great combination of cheese, eggs, veggies, and meat. This richly meaty omelet will surely impress your family.

Serves 2 | Prep time 15 minutes | Cooking time 12 minutes

Ingredients
1 tablespoon butter
¼ cup bell pepper, seeded and chopped
¼ cup onions, chopped
¼ cup ham, chopped
4 eggs, beaten
2 tablespoons water
¼ teaspoon salt
1 teaspoon olive oil
¼ cup tomatoes, chopped
⅓ cup cooked beef, finely chopped
¼ cup cooked bacon, chopped
⅓ cup cooked breakfast sausage, chopped
¾ cup Cheddar cheese, shredded

Directions
1. In a skillet, melt the butter over medium-low heat and sauté the bell pepper and onion for 4–5 minutes.
2. Add the ham and cook for 2–3 minutes or until heated through.
3. Immediately remove from the heat and set aside.
4. In a bowl, beat the eggs with water and salt.
5. In a 12-inch frying pan, heat the oil over medium-low heat.
6. Add the egg mixture and sprinkle with the cooked ham mixture, tomato, beef, sausage, bacon, and cheese.
7. Cook for 2–3 minutes or until the omelet starts to set.
8. Fold the omelet in half.
9. Transfer the omelet to a plate and serve hot.

Nutrition (per serving)
Calories 613, fat 46.6 g, carbs 4.9 g, sugar 2.4 g, Protein 42.8 g, sodium 1130 mg

Cheese Omelet (Waffle House)

This three-ingredient omelet is a really great option for egg and cheese lovers. Kids especially will love to enjoy this breakfast.

Serves 1 | Prep time 10 minutes | Cooking time 5 minutes

Ingredients
3 large eggs
2 tablespoons olive oil
2 slices American cheese

Directions
1. In a bowl, beat the eggs for about 1 minute.
2. In a skillet, heat the oil over high heat.
3. Slowly add the beaten eggs, moving the skillet continuously in a circular motion.
4. Cook until the outside edges are set, moving the skillet continuously in a circular motion.

5. Carefully flip the omelet and cook for about 30 seconds, moving the skillet occasionally in a circular motion.
6. Arrange the cheese slices over the center of the omelet.
7. Fold the omelet in half to cover the cheese slices.
8. Transfer to a serving plate.

Nutrition (per serving)
Calories 548, fat 50.1 g, carbs 3 g, sugar 3 g,
Protein 24.1 g, sodium 581 mg

Egg Bites (Starbucks)

One of the best recipes for muffins with bacon, eggs, and cheese. These egg bites are the best make-ahead breakfast recipe for healthy eating.

Serves 6 | Prep time 10 minutes | Cooking time 30 minutes

Ingredients
½ cup Swiss cheese, shredded
¼ cup full-fat cottage cheese
5 eggs
¼ teaspoon salt
Pepper to taste
2 thick bacon slices, cooked and chopped

Directions
1. Preheat the oven to 300°F.
2. Add about 1 inch of water to a baking dish.
3. Place the baking dish on the bottom rack of the oven while preheating.

4. Grease 6 cups of a muffin tin.
5. In a blender, pulse the Swiss cheese, cottage cheese, eggs, salt, and pepper on high speed until light and frothy.
6. Divide the cheese mixture among the prepared muffin cups.
7. Divide the bacon into each cup and stir gently to combine.
8. Bake for about 30 minutes or until the tops turn golden brown.
9. Remove the muffin pan from the oven and place it on a wire rack to cool for about 5 minutes.
10. Carefully invert the muffins onto a platter and serve warm.

Nutrition (per serving)
Calories 147, fat 10.4 g, carbs 1.3 g, sugar 0.4 g,
Protein 11.9 g, sodium 427 mg

Breakfast Soufflé
(Panera Bread)

Make your breakfast table amazing with cheese soufflé! This soufflé is packed with delicious spinach, bacon, eggs, cream, and cheese.

Serves 4 | Prep time 20 minutes | Cooking time 26 minutes

Ingredients
Puff Pastry
¼ cup almond flour
1 tablespoon coconut flour
5 tablespoons psyllium husks
¼ teaspoon baking powder
1 teaspoon xanthan gum
⅛ teaspoon salt
½ cup cold butter, chopped
1 egg white
½ cup cold water

Soufflé
3 large eggs
¼ cup Parmesan cheese, finely grated
2 tablespoons sour cream
1–2 dashes hot sauce
½ teaspoon baking powder
¼ teaspoon garlic powder
¼ teaspoon salt
¼ cup cooked bacon, chopped
¼ cup frozen chopped spinach, thawed
¼ cup Asiago cheese, grated

Directions
1. For the pastry, in a food processor, pulse the flours, psyllium husks, baking powder, xanthan gum, and salt into a fine powder.
2. Add the butter and pulse until coated.
3. Transfer the mixture to a bowl.
4. Add the egg white and cold water and mix with a spoon until a rough dough forms.
5. Knead to form a dough ball.
6. Cover the dough ball with plastic wrap and refrigerate for about 30 minutes.
7. Preheat the oven to 400°F.
8. For the soufflé, in a bowl, beat the eggs lightly.
9. Add the Parmesan cheese, sour cream, hot sauce, baking powder, garlic powder, and salt and mix well.
10. Add the spinach and bacon and stir to combine.
11. Place the dough between 2 lightly floured sheets of parchment paper and roll it out with a rolling pin.
12. Refrigerate until ready to use.
13. Cut the dough into four squares.
14. Place the pastry squares in the bottoms of four 4-inch tart pans and press slightly.
15. Divide the spinach mixture among the pans and sprinkle with Asiago cheese.
16. Bake for 24–26 minutes or until the eggs are puffy.

Nutrition (per serving)
Calories 478, fat 14.1 g, carbs 10 g, sugar 0.9 g,
Protein 15.7 g, sodium 737 mg

Hash Brown Casserole (Cracker Barrel)

A filling and delicious casserole for breakfast. This keto-friendly casserole is loaded with cauliflower, cheese, cream, and mayonnaise.

Serves 8 | Prep time 15 minutes | Cooking time 1 hour

Ingredients
2 cup shredded cheddar and Monterey jack cheese, divided
3 cups cauliflower florets, cut small
1 tablespoon onion, minced
1 cup sour cream
½ cup mayonnaise
¼ cup butter, softened
1 tablespoon bouillon powder
1 teaspoon salt
½ teaspoon pepper

Directions
1. Preheat the oven to 350°F.
2. Grease an 8×8-inch baking dish.
3. In a bowl, stir together 1 cup of cheese and the remaining ingredients.
4. Place the mixture in the prepared baking dish and sprinkle it with the remaining cheese.
5. Bake for 50–60 minutes until the top is golden and bubbly.
6. Serve hot.

Nutrition (per serving)
Calories 324, fat 31 g, carbs 3.8 g, sugar 1.1 g,
Protein 8.2 g, sodium 626 mg

Chonaga Everything Bagel (Starbucks)

The best-ever recipe for bagels that you can prepare at home easily. The combo of mozzarella cheese and cream cheese gives a flavorsome texture.

Serves 6 | Prep time 15 minutes | Cooking time 10 minutes

Ingredients
2 cups almond flour
1 tablespoon baking powder
1 teaspoon dried Italian seasoning
1 teaspoon onion powder
1 teaspoon garlic powder
3 cups low-moisture mozzarella cheese, shredded
5 tablespoons cream cheese
3 large eggs, divided
3 tablespoons Everything Bagel Seasoning

Directions
1. Preheat the oven to 425°F. Arrange the rack in the middle.
2. Line a rimmed baking sheet with parchment paper.
3. In a bowl, sift together the almond flour, baking powder, Italian seasoning, onion powder, and garlic powder.
4. In a large microwave-safe bowl, microwave the mozzarella cheese and cream cheese for about 2½ minutes, stirring once after 1½ minutes.
5. Remove from microwave and stir until smooth.
6. Add 2 eggs and the flour mixture and mix well.
7. Divide the dough into 6 pieces and shape each piece into a ball.
8. Gently press your finger into the center of each dough ball to form a small hole.
9. In a small bowl, lightly beat the remaining egg.
10. Brush the top of each bagel with beaten egg and sprinkle with Everything Bagel Seasoning.
11. Arrange the bagels on the prepared baking sheet.
12. Bake for 12–14 minutes or until golden brown.
13. Serve warm.

Nutrition (per serving)
Calories 355, fat 29 g, carbs 9.5 g, sugar 1.9 g,
Protein 7.8 g, sodium 211 mg

Waffles (Waffle House)

A super recipe that is easily prepared with ingredients that everyone has on hand. This recipe makes exceptionally delicious waffles for breakfast.

Serves 4 | Prep time 10 minutes | Cooking time 25 minutes

Ingredients
5 medium eggs, whites, and yolks separated
¼ cup coconut flour
¼ cup granulated erythritol
1 teaspoon baking powder
½ cup butter, melted
3 tablespoons cream
2 teaspoons vanilla extract

Directions
1. In a clean glass bowl, beat the egg whites until stiff peaks form.
2. In another bowl, mix the flour, erythritol, baking powder, and egg yolks until well combined.
3. Slowly add the melted butter, beating continuously until smooth.
4. Add the cream and vanilla and mix well.
5. Gently fold in the whipped egg whites.
6. Place an appropriate amount of the mixture in a preheated waffle iron and cook for 4–5 minutes or until golden brown.
7. Repeat with the remaining mixture.
8. Serve warm.

Nutrition (per serving)
Calories 260, fat 23.8 g, carbs 5.3 g, sugar 0.7 g,
Protein 6.6 g, sodium 196 mg

Wild Blueberry Muffins (Panera Bread)

A hit recipe for those days when fresh blueberries are in season. These light and fruity muffins are a classic choice for breakfast.

*Serves 12 | Prep time 10 minutes
Cooking time 25 minutes*

Ingredients
Muffins
3½ cups almond meal
3–4 tablespoons granulated erythritol
2 teaspoons baking powder
6 medium eggs
1¼ cups plain full-fat yogurt
¼ cup butter, melted
2 teaspoons vanilla extract

½ cup fresh wild blueberries

Topping
¾ cup erythritol
¾ cup almond flour
½ cup cold butter, chopped

Directions
1. Preheat the oven to 350°F.
2. Line a 12-cup muffin tin with paper liners.
3. To make the muffins, in a bowl, mix together the flour, erythritol, and baking powder.
4. In another bowl, beat the eggs, yogurt, butter, and vanilla until well combined.
5. Add the flour mixture and mix until just combined.
6. Gently fold in the blueberries.
7. To make the topping, in a bowl, mix all of the ingredients until a crumbly mixture forms.
8. Transfer the batter mixture into the prepared muffin cups and sprinkle each with a topping mixture.
9. Bake for about 25 minutes or until a toothpick inserted in the center comes out clean.
10. Remove the muffin tin from the oven and place it on a wire rack to cool for about 10 minutes.
11. Carefully invert the muffins onto the wire rack to cool completely before serving.

Nutrition (per serving)
Calories 398, fat 34 g, carbs 9 g, sugar 3.9 g,
Protein 4 g, sodium 129 mg

Lemon Poppy Seed Bread (Starbucks)

A versatile bread with the flavor of super-healthy lemon and poppy seeds. You will surely find this lemony bread really delicious.

*Serves 14 | Prep time 15 minutes
Cooking time 30 minutes*

Ingredients
2 cups almond flour
⅓ cup erythritol
1 teaspoon poppy seeds
1 teaspoon baking powder
2 eggs
¼ cup butter, melted

¼ cup sour cream
2 tablespoons lemon juice
1 teaspoon lemon extract
1 teaspoon lemon zest

Directions
1. Preheat the oven to 350°F.
2. Line a loaf pan with parchment paper.
3. In a bowl, mix together the flour, erythritol, poppy seeds, and baking powder.
4. Add the remaining ingredients and mix well.
5. Place the dough in the prepared loaf pan.
6. Bake for about 30 minutes or until a toothpick inserted in the center comes out clean.
7. Remove the loaf pan from the oven and place on a wire rack for about 10 minutes.
8. Carefully invert the bread loaf onto the wire rack to cool completely before serving.
9. Slice and serve.

Nutrition (per serving)
Calories 150, fat 13.3 g, carbs 3.4 g, sugar 0.7 g, Protein 1 g, sodium 35 mg

Pumpkin Bread (Starbucks)

An excellent recipe for pumpkin bread for breakfast. This bread is packed with the flavors of pumpkin, coconut oil, and butter.

Serves 10 | Prep time 10 minutes | Cooking time 1¼ hours

Ingredients
½ cup + 2 teaspoons coconut flour
1½ teaspoons baking powder
4 teaspoons pumpkin pie spice
½ teaspoon salt
5 eggs
1½ cups powdered erythritol
1 cup sugar-free pumpkin puree
½ cup coconut oil, melted
2 tablespoons butter, melted
1 teaspoon vanilla extract

Directions
1. Preheat the oven to 350°F.
2. Line a 9×5-inch loaf pan with parchment paper.
3. In a bowl, sift together coconut flour, baking powder, pumpkin pie spice mix, and salt.
4. In another bowl, beat the eggs, erythritol, pumpkin puree, coconut oil, butter, and vanilla.
5. Add the flour mixture and mix until just combined.
6. Place the dough into the prepared loaf pan.
7. Bake for about 1¼ hours or until a toothpick inserted in the center comes out clean.
8. Remove the loaf pan from the oven and place on a wire rack for about 10 minutes.
9. Carefully invert the bread onto the wire rack to cool completely before serving.
10. Slice and serve.

Nutrition (per serving)
Calories 182, fat 16.2 g, carbs 7 g, sugar 1.1 g,
Protein 3.9 g, sodium 166 mg

McGriddle Sandwich (McDonald's)

The McGriddle sandwich is a breakfast sandwich packed with homemade pancakes. These sandwiches are flavored with eggs, cheese, sausage, and bacon.

Serves 2 | Prep time 15 minutes | Cooking time 28 minutes

Ingredients
Pancakes
¾ cup almond flour
1 teaspoon baking powder
½ teaspoon salt
4 ounces cream cheese, softened
2 large eggs
1 tablespoon powdered erythritol
1 teaspoon vanilla extract
2 tablespoons butter

Filling
1 tablespoon butter (divided)
3 large eggs, beaten
2 slices cheddar cheese
2 cooked breakfast sausage patties
4 slices cooked bacon

Directions
1. For the pancakes, in a bowl, mix together the flour, baking powder, and salt.
2. In another large bowl, beat the cream cheese, eggs, erythritol, and vanilla with a hand mixer until fluffy.
3. Add the flour mixture and mix until smooth.
4. In a skillet, melt ½ tablespoon of the butter over medium heat.
5. Add about ¼ cup of the mixture and cook for 1–2 minutes per side.
6. Cook for another 2–3 minutes or until completely done.
7. Repeat with the remaining butter and mixture.

8. Meanwhile, make the filling in a frying pan, melt ½ tablespoon of butter and cook half of the beaten eggs for 3–4 minutes or until desired doneness.
9. Fold the omelet and remove from heat.
10. Repeat with the remaining butter and eggs.
11. Arrange 2 pancakes on serving plates.
12. Top each pancake with 1 cheese slice, followed by omelet, sausage patty, and bacon slices.
13. Cover with the remaining pancakes and serve.

Nutrition (per serving)
Calories 973, fat 50 g, carbs 29.3 g, sugar 2 g,
Protein 57 g, sodium 1200 mg

KETO COPYCAT APPETIZER AND SNACK RECIPES

Artichoke-Spinach Dip (Olive Garden)

A rich and creamy dip for your snack table. This baked spinach artichoke dip recipe is full of the best flavors and extra-easy to make.

Serves 10 | Prep time 10 minutes | Cooking time 20 minutes

Ingredients
1 (8-ounce) package cream cheese, softened
¼ cup Romano cheese, shredded
¼ cup Parmesan cheese, shredded
¼ cup mayonnaise
1 clove garlic, finely minced
½ teaspoon dried basil
¼ teaspoon garlic salt
Salt and pepper to taste
1 (14-ounce) can artichoke hearts, drained and roughly chopped
½ cup frozen chopped spinach
¼ cup mozzarella cheese, grated

Directions
1. Preheat the oven to 350°F.
2. In a bowl, mix together the cream cheese, Romano cheese, Parmesan cheese, mayonnaise, garlic, basil, garlic salt, salt, and pepper.
3. Mix in the artichoke hearts and spinach.
4. Place the cheese mixture in a greased pie dish and sprinkle with mozzarella cheese.
5. Bake for about 25 minutes or until the top is browned.
6. Serve hot.

Nutrition (per serving)
Calories 272, fat 25.2 g, carbs 5.3 g, sugar 0.5 g, Protein 7.5 g, sodium 222 mg

Queso Blanco (Applebee's)

A restaurant-quality dip that is easily prepared at home. This dip will surely be a great addition to your menu list.

Serves 10 | Prep time 10 minutes | Cooking time 15 minutes

Ingredients
2 tablespoons olive oil
⅓ cup white onion, finely chopped
2 tablespoons jalapeño pepper, finely minced
1 pound white American cheese, cut into large pieces
½ pound Monterey Jack cheese, cut into large pieces
½ cup half-and-half
⅓–½ cup tomatoes, chopped
2 tablespoons fresh cilantro, chopped (divided)
1 jalapeño pepper, chopped

Directions
1. In a medium pan, heat the oil over medium-low heat and sauté the onion and jalapeño for 2–3 minutes.
2. Add the cheeses and half-and-half and stir to combine.
3. Reduce heat to low and cook for 2–3 minutes or until the cheeses are melted.
4. Add the tomato pieces and stir to combine.
5. Stir in half of the cilantro and remove from heat.
6. Serve garnished with the remaining cilantro and chopped jalapeño.

Nutrition (per serving)
Calories 277, fat 22.5 g, carbs 4.9 g, sugar 3.9 g, Protein 2 g, sodium 701 mg

Lettuce Wraps (PF Chang)

When you want a super delicious snacking treat that's different from the usual, these wraps hit the spot. Ground turkey and veggies get a flavorsome taste with a sweet and savory sauce.

Serves 8 | Prep time 15 minutes | Cooking time 10 minutes

Ingredients
Sauce
3 tablespoons low-sodium soy sauce
1 tablespoon balsamic vinegar
1 tablespoon sesame oil
1 tablespoon almond butter
1 tablespoon erythritol
2 cloves garlic, minced
½ teaspoon ginger paste

Lettuce Wraps
1 tablespoon olive oil
1 pound ground turkey
2 teaspoons dried minced onion

¼ teaspoon salt
¼ teaspoon pepper
3 ounces shiitake mushrooms, chopped
½ cup carrot, peeled and chopped
3 scallions, thinly sliced
1 head butter lettuce

Directions
1. Beat all of the sauce ingredients in a bowl until well combined.
2. In a skillet, heat the olive oil over medium heat and cook the ground turkey for 4–5 minutes.
3. Stir in the onion, salt, and pepper, and cook for 1–2 minutes.
4. Stir in the mushrooms, carrot, and scallions and cook for 5–6 minutes, stirring frequently.
5. Add the sauce and stir to combine.
6. Remove from heat and set aside to cool slightly.
7. Arrange the lettuce leaves on serving plates.
8. Place some turkey mixture over each lettuce leaf and serve.

Nutrition (per serving)
Calories 247, fat 27.7 g, carbs 7 g, sugar 0 g,
Protein 1.4 g, sodium 219 mg

Bloomin' Onion
(Outback Steakhouse)

An absolutely amazing snack recipe. You will surely love to enjoy this delicious restaurant-quality bloomin' onion.

Serves 4 | Prep time 15 minutes | Cooking time 5 minutes

Ingredients
Dipping sauce
¾ cup sour cream
5–10 dashes hot sauce
1 teaspoon paprika
½ teaspoon onion powder
Salt to taste

Onion
1 large sweet onion
½ cup coconut flour
¼ cup heavy whipping cream
4 eggs
1 cup pork rind, crushed
½ tablespoon seasoning salt
½ tablespoon cayenne pepper
½ tablespoon paprika
½ teaspoon pepper

Directions
1. Beat all of the sauce ingredients in a bowl until well combined. Refrigerate until ready to use.
2. Cut off the top of the onion and remove the skin.
3. With a sharp knife, make four ½-inch cuts then make three cuts in each quarter.
4. Flip the onion, so it is open, then cut off the center petals.
5. Sprinkle the onion with coconut flour, separating the petals to coat the entire onion.
6. In a small bowl, mix the heavy cream and eggs.
7. In another bowl, mix together the pork rinds and spices.
8. Pour about half of the egg mixture over the onion to coat the entire onion.
9. Coat the onion evenly with the pork rind mixture.
10. Pour the remaining egg mixture over the onion.
11. Place the onion in the freezer for 1 hour.
12. Fill a large, heavy-bottomed pan about ⅔ of the way full with olive oil.
13. Heat over medium heat.
14. Carefully place the onion in the hot oil, petal side down, and cook for about 1 minute.
15. Reduce heat to medium-low.
16. Carefully flip the onion and cook for about 2–3 minutes.
17. Serve immediately alongside the dipping sauce.

Nutrition (per serving)
Calories 275, fat 22 g, carbs 7.6 g, sugar 2.3 g,
Protein 12.8 g, sodium 853 mg

Chicken Nuggets (Burger King)

An awesome kid-friendly recipe that will also become an adult's favorite. These nuggets will surely be a great choice for the party's snack menu.

Serves 6 | Prep time 10 minutes | Cooking time 20 minutes

Ingredients
2 large eggs
1 cup almond flour
1 tablespoon smoked paprika
1 tablespoon celery salt
½ teaspoon garlic powder
½ teaspoon onion powder
1 teaspoon salt
½ teaspoon pepper
1 pound boneless, skinless chicken breast fillets, cut into bite-sized pieces

Directions
1. Preheat the oven to 400°F.
2. Line a large baking sheet with parchment paper.
3. In a shallow dish, beat the eggs.
4. In another shallow dish, mix together the flour and spices.
5. Dip the chicken pieces into the beaten eggs and then coat with the flour mixture.
6. Arrange the chicken pieces on the prepared baking sheet in a single layer.
7. Bake for 20–22 minutes, flipping once halfway through.
8. Serve warm.

Nutrition (per serving)
Calories 236, fat 13.7 g, carbs 4.6 g, sugar 1.1 g,
Protein 18.4 g, sodium 455 mg

Buffalo Wings
(Cheesecake Factory)

One of the easiest and most delicious ways to prepare chicken wings. These wings will surely be a huge hit with both kids and adults.

Serves 6 | Prep time 15 minutes | Cooking time 36 minutes

Ingredients
2 pounds whole chicken wings
Salt and pepper to taste
½ cup butter (divided)
2 tablespoons olive oil
½ cup taco sauce
¼ cup sugar-free barbecue sauce
¼ cup French salad dressing
1 teaspoon Worcestershire sauce

⅛ teaspoon hot pepper sauce

Directions
1. Preheat the oven to 325°F.
2. Cut each chicken wing into three sections and discard the wingtips.
3. Season the wings with salt and pepper.
4. In a skillet, heat 2 tablespoons of butter and the oil over medium heat and fry the wings for 6–8 minutes per side or until browned.
5. Meanwhile, in a saucepan, cook the remaining butter, taco sauce, barbecue sauce, French dressing, Worcestershire sauce, and hot pepper sauce over medium heat until the butter is melted and the sauce is well combined, stirring continuously.
6. Place the chicken wings in a greased 13×9-inch baking dish.
7. Pour ½ cup of sauce over the chicken wings.
8. Bake for about 15–20 minutes.
9. Serve hot with the remaining sauce.

Nutrition (per serving)
Calories 489, fat 31.4 g, carbs 5.8 g, sugar 3.5 g, Protein 44.2 g, sodium 498 mg

Turkey Lettuce Wrap (Jimmy John's)

A super delicious and filling lettuce wrap recipe. Turkey, cheese, mayonnaise, mustard, and veggies make a wonderful filling for lettuce.

Serves 2 | Prep time 15 minutes

Ingredients
2–3 large iceberg lettuce leaves
2 (1-ounce) turkey slices
2 cheese provolone slices
½ small avocado, peeled, pitted, and sliced

6 cucumber slices
4 tomato slices
1 tablespoon mayonnaise
1 tablespoon yellow mustard
Pinch of salt
Pinch of pepper

Directions
1. Arrange the lettuce leaves on a smooth surface in an overlapping row.
2. Place the remaining ingredients over the lettuce in layers, closer to the bottom half of the lettuce.
3. Roll the leaves tightly and serve.

Nutrition (per serving)
Calories 406, fat 28.9 g, carbs 8.5 g, sugar 1.9 g,
Protein 29.3 g, sodium 660 mg

Green Beans Crisper (Applebee's)

An impressive and easy recipe for delicious green bean crispers. Lemony flavored aioli complements green beans nicely.

Serves 4 | Prep time 15 minutes | Cooking time 16 minutes

Ingredients
Green beans
1 pound fresh green beans, washed, ends trimmed
1 cup almond flour
1½ cups white wine
1–2 cups olive oil
Salt and pepper to taste

Lemon-garlic aioli
½ cup mayonnaise
1 tablespoon lemon juice

½ teaspoon lemon zest, grated
1 teaspoon mustard powder
½ teaspoon garlic powder
Salt and pepper to taste

Directions
1. Add all of the aioli ingredients to a bowl and mix until creamy. Refrigerate until ready to serve.
2. In a large bowl, mix the flour and wine until smooth.
3. Coat the green beans with the flour mixture.
4. In a deep skillet, heat the oil over medium-high heat and fry the green beans in 4 batches for 2–4 minutes.
5. With a slotted spoon, transfer the beans onto a paper-towel-lined plate to drain.
6. Sprinkle with salt and pepper and serve warm with the lemon-garlic aioli.

Nutrition (per serving)
Calories 900, fat 85.7 g, carbs 13.7 g, sugar 4.8 g, Protein 1.8 g, sodium 239 mg

Cheddar Bay Biscuit (Red Lobster)

One of the best cheesy biscuits, with a wonderful aroma and texture. These amazing cheesy biscuits are also rich in taste.

Serves 8 | Prep time 15 minutes | Cooking time 11 minutes

Ingredients
Biscuits
1½ cups superfine almond flour
1 tablespoon baking powder
½ teaspoon garlic powder
½ teaspoon onion powder
¼ teaspoon salt
½ cup sour cream
¼ cup unsalted butter, melted
2 large eggs
½ cup cheddar cheese, shredded

<u>Topping</u>
2 tablespoons butter, melted
1 tablespoon fresh parsley, minced
½ teaspoon garlic powder

Directions
1. Preheat the oven to 450°F.
2. Lightly grease 9 cups of a muffin pan.
3. In a large bowl, mix together the almond flour, baking powder, and seasoning.
4. In a small bowl, beat the sour cream, butter, and eggs until smooth.
5. Add the egg mixture to the flour bowl and mix well.
6. Gently fold in the cheese.
7. Divide the mixture into the prepared muffin cups.
8. Bake for about 10–11 minutes or until the tops turn golden.
9. Meanwhile, mix together the butter, parsley, and garlic powder in a bowl.
10. Brush the tops of the hot biscuits with the butter mixture.
11. Serve warm.

Nutrition (per serving)
Calories 259, fat 23.6 g, carbs 5 g, sugar 0.9 g,
Protein 3.5 g, sodium 184 mg

Fried Mozzarella (Olive Garden)

A delicious cheesy snack that is light in texture but rich in taste. You will surely receive huge appreciation after preparing this snack.

Serves 4 | Prep time 15 minutes | Cooking time 6 minutes

Ingredients
⅔ cup almond flour
⅓ cup arrowroot starch
2 eggs, beaten
¼ cup water
1½ cups pork rinds, finely crushed
1 teaspoon Italian seasoning
½ teaspoons garlic salt
1 pound mozzarella cheese, cut into thick slices
1–2 cups olive oil

Directions
1. In a shallow bowl, mix together the flour and arrowroot starch.
2. In a second shallow bowl, lightly beat the eggs and water.
3. In a third shallow bowl, mix together the pork rinds, Italian seasoning, and garlic salt.
4. Coat the mozzarella slices with the flour mixture, then dip them into the egg mixture, and finally coat them with the pork rind mixture.
5. In a deep skillet, heat the oil over medium heat and fry the mozzarella slices in 3 batches for about 1 minute per side.
6. With a slotted spoon, transfer the mozzarella sticks onto a paper-towel-lined plate to drain.
7. Serve warm.

Nutrition (per serving)
Calories 679, fat 68.2 g, carbs 5.5 g, sugar 1 g,
Protein 12.5 g, sodium 294 mg

KETO COPYCAT SALAD AND SOUP RECIPES

Green Goddess Cobb Salad (Panera Bread)

A salad recipe with a bunch of delish ingredients. This recipe is also a great choice to make a salad for a crowd in a short time.

Serves 2 | Prep time 15 minutes | Cooking time 10 minutes

Ingredients
Dressing
½ cup mayonnaise
½ cup watercress, cleaned and tough stems removed

½ cup fresh parsley, minced
2 tablespoons fresh tarragon leaves
1 tablespoon fresh chives, minced
2 tablespoons lemon juice
1 tablespoon balsamic vinegar
½ teaspoon salt
¼ teaspoon pepper

Salad
6 ounces grilled chicken breast, sliced
2 tablespoons cooked bacon, chopped
1 hard-boiled egg, sliced
6 ounces salad blend
½ cup tomatoes, chopped
2 tablespoons onion, chopped
3 tablespoons avocado, peeled, pitted, and chopped
2 tablespoons feta cheese, crumbled

Directions
1. Add all the dressing ingredients to a food processor and pulse until smooth and creamy.
2. Divide the salad ingredients onto serving plates.
3. Drizzle with dressing and serve.

Nutrition (per serving)
Calories 648, fat 54.7 g, carbs 8.7 g, sugar 2.8 g,
Protein 29.4 g, sodium 888 mg

Coleslaw (KFC)

A simple and easy creamy salad recipe that the whole family will enjoy. This salad is a great combo of mayonnaise, almond milk, cabbage, and carrot.

Serves 8 | Prep time 10 minutes

Ingredients
¾ cup vegan mayonnaise
¼ cup unsweetened almond milk
3 tablespoons white vinegar
1 tablespoon lemon juice
¼ cup erythritol
1 tablespoon onion powder
Salt and ground white pepper to taste
1 head green cabbage, chopped
1 carrot, peeled and chopped

Directions
1. In a bowl, mix the mayonnaise, almond milk, vinegar, lemon juice, erythritol, onion powder, salt, and white pepper until well combined.
2. In a salad bowl, mix the cabbage and carrot.
3. Add the dressing and toss to coat well.
4. Cover and refrigerate for at least 2–3 hours before serving.

Nutrition (per serving)
Calories 166, fat 15.2 g, carbs 6.8 g, sugar 3.6 g,
Protein 1.3 g, sodium 163 mg

Cucumber Tomato Salad (Cracker Barrel)

One of the best salads with a refreshing touch of dressing. This tangy dressing complements the crunchy veggies nicely.

Serves 6 | Prep time 15 minutes

Ingredients
1 cup white vinegar
½ cup erythritol
2 tablespoons Italian dressing
1 pound tomatoes, chopped
3 cucumbers, chopped
½ cup white onion, sliced

Directions
1. In a large bowl, mix the vinegar, erythritol, and Italian dressing until well combined.
2. Add the remaining ingredients and toss to coat well.
3. Cover and refrigerate for about 1 hour before serving.

Nutrition (per serving)
Calories 63, fat 1.7 g, carbs 10 g, sugar 5 g,
Protein 1.8 g, sodium 11 mg

Salad (Olive Garden)

A lovely bowl of colors and flavors. The Italian dressing makes a perfect match for the fresh veggies.

Serves 6 | Prep time 15 minutes

Ingredients
6 ounces iceberg lettuce
6 ounces fresh baby greens
2 small tomatoes, sliced
12 black olives, pitted
¼ small onion, sliced
6 mild pepperoncini peppers
½ cup Italian dressing
Pepper to taste
¼ cup Parmesan cheese, grated

Directions
1. Add all of the ingredients to a salad bowl and toss to coat well.
2. Serve immediately.

Nutrition (per serving)
Calories 108, fat 7.4 g, carbs 9 g, sugar 3.8 g,
Protein 2.9 g, sodium 403 mg

Cobb Salad
(Cheesecake Factory)

A fresh and delicious way to enjoy the excellent flavors of chicken, eggs, bacon, tomato, and avocado. This delicious salad is very bright and hearty.

Serves 6 | Prep time 15 minutes

Ingredients
Dressing
1 cup olive oil
¼ cup red wine vinegar
1 teaspoon lemon juice
¾ teaspoon Worcestershire sauce
1 small garlic clove, minced
¼ teaspoon erythritol
¼ teaspoon ground mustard
Salt and pepper to taste

<u>Salad</u>
2 cooked chicken breasts, chopped
6 cooked bacon strips, crumbled
6½ cups romaine lettuce, torn
2½ cups curly endive, torn
4 ounces fresh watercress, trimmed and chopped
2 medium tomatoes, seeded and chopped
1 medium ripe avocado, peeled, pitted, and chopped
3 hard-boiled large eggs, peeled and chopped
½ cup blue cheese, crumbled
2 tablespoons fresh chives, minced

Directions
1. In a blender, pulse all of the dressing ingredients until smooth.
2. Transfer the dressing to a bowl and refrigerate before serving.
3. In a large salad bowl, mix all of the salad ingredients.
4. Cover and refrigerate to chill before serving.
5. Just before serving, drizzle the salad with the dressing.

Nutrition (per serving)
Calories 680, fat 60 g, carbs 7 g, sugar 1.9 g,
Protein 32 g, sodium 919 mg

Zuppa Toscana (Olive Garden)

A traditional Italian soup recipe. This soup is packed with flavor from crispy bacon, Italian sausage, spinach, and tender cauliflower.

Serves 6 | Prep time 15 minutes | Cooking time 30 minutes

Ingredients
1 pound mild Italian sausage, sliced
4 thick-cut bacon slices, chopped
1 head cauliflower, chopped
1 small onion, chopped
3 cloves garlic, minced
1 quart beef broth
2 cups fresh spinach
½ cup heavy whipping cream
Salt and pepper to taste

Directions
1. Heat a large Dutch oven over medium heat and cook the beef and bacon for 6–8 minutes or until browned.
2. Stir in the cauliflower, onions, garlic, and broth, and bring to a boil.
3. Cover and cook for about 15 minutes.
4. Stir in the spinach and heavy cream and cook for about 5 minutes.
5. Stir in the salt and pepper and remove from heat.
6. Serve hot.

Nutrition (per serving)
Calories 440, fat 32.4 g, carbs 5.4 g, sugar 2.1 g, Protein 26.5 g, sodium 1320 mg

Egg Drop Soup
(Chinese Imperial Place)

This easy Chinese egg drop soup is ready in just 20 minutes. This soup tastes just like the soup at your favorite Chinese restaurant!

Serves 6 | Prep time 10 minutes | Cooking time 10 minutes

Ingredients
1 egg
2 teaspoons toasted sesame oil (divided)
1½ quarts chicken broth
Salt to taste
¼ teaspoon ground white pepper
3 scallion greens, sliced

Directions
1. In a small bowl, slightly beat the egg with 1 teaspoon of sesame oil. Set aside.
2. Add the broth to a pan and bring to a boil over medium-low heat.
3. Slowly stir in the egg mixture.
4. Stir in the remaining sesame oil, salt, and white pepper.
5. Simmer for 4–5 minutes or until soup reaches the desired thickness, stirring continuously.
6. Serve hot garnished with scallions.

Nutrition (per serving)
Calories 65, fat 3.6 g, carbs 1.6 g, sugar 0.9 g, Protein 5.9 g, sodium 802 mg

Broccoli Cheddar Soup (Panera Bread)

A greatly flavored and delicious broccoli soup with a rich cheesy touch. This soup will be a hit at gatherings of family and friends.

Serves 4 | Prep time 15 minutes | Cooking time 15 minutes

Ingredients
¼ cup butter
½ onion, chopped
2–3 cloves garlic, minced
3 cups broccoli florets
1 teaspoon spicy mustard
¼ teaspoon ground nutmeg
½ teaspoon paprika
½ teaspoon pepper
3 cups chicken broth

1 cup heavy cream
1 teaspoon xanthan gum
Salt to taste
½ pound cheddar cheese, grated

Directions
1. In a Dutch oven, melt the butter over medium heat and sauté the onion for 2–3 minutes.
2. Add the garlic and sauté for about 1 minute.
3. Add the broccoli, mustard, nutmeg, paprika, and pepper and stir to combine.
4. Reduce heat to medium-low and simmer, covered, for about 10 minutes.
5. Add the cream, xanthan gum, and salt and stir to combine.
6. Remove from heat and stir in the cheddar cheese until melted completely.
7. Serve hot.

Nutrition (per serving)
Calories 498, fat 42.8 g, carbs 8 g, sugar 2.7 g,
Protein 20.7 g, sodium 1000 mg

Mushroom Truffle Bisque (Longhorn Steakhouse)

A delicious and nourishing mushroom soup. Fresh mushrooms, heavy cream, and truffle oil combine nicely.

Serves 4 | Prep time 15 minutes | Cooking time 15 minutes

Ingredients
2 tablespoons butter
4 ounces fresh baby Portobello mushroom, sliced
4 ounces fresh white button mushrooms, sliced
½ cup yellow onion, chopped
½ teaspoon salt
1 teaspoon garlic, chopped
3 cups chicken broth
1 cup heavy cream
1½ teaspoons truffle oil

Directions
1. In a medium pan, melt the butter over medium heat.
2. Cook the mushrooms and onion with salt for 5–7 minutes, stirring frequently.
3. Add the garlic and sauté for 1–2 minutes.
4. Stir in the broth and remove from heat.
5. With a stick blender, blend the soup until the mushrooms are chopped very finely.
6. Add the heavy cream and stir to combine.
7. Place the pan over medium heat and cook for 3–5 minutes.
8. Remove from heat and stir in the truffle oil.
9. Serve immediately.

Nutrition (per serving)
Calories 217, fat 19.8 g, carbs 5 g, sugar 2.1 g,
Protein 6.3 g, sodium 919 mg

Tomato Basil Soup (Applebee's)

A quite comforting and delicious soup. Basil adds a refreshingly tasty touch to this tomato soup.

Serves 8 | Prep time 15 minutes | Cooking time 30 minutes

Ingredients
1 tablespoon olive oil
½ cup white onion, chopped
2 cloves garlic, minced
2 (28-ounce) cans sugar-free crushed tomatoes
2½ cups chicken broth
1 tablespoon erythritol

¾ cup heavy cream
¼ cup fresh basil, minced
1½ teaspoons dried parsley
½ teaspoon dried oregano
Salt to taste
¼ teaspoon pepper

Directions
1. In a large soup pan, heat the olive oil over medium heat and sauté the onion for 2–3 minutes.
2. Add the garlic and sauté for about 1 minute.
3. Add the tomatoes, broth, and erythritol and bring to a boil.
4. Cook, uncovered, for about 20 minutes.
5. With an immersion blender, blend the soup until smooth.
6. Stir in the heavy cream and herbs and bring to a gentle simmer over medium heat.
7. Reduce heat to low and simmer for about 5 minutes, stirring occasionally.
8. Stir in the salt and pepper and remove from heat.
9. Serve hot garnished with extra basil leaves.

Nutrition (per serving)
Calories 106, fat 6.8 g, carbs 9 g, sugar 5 g,
Protein 3.7 g, sodium 253 mg

KETO COPYCAT CHICKEN RECIPES

Chicken Pot Pie (Cracker Barrel)

A comforting and flavorsome chicken and veggie-filled pastry. This double crust chicken pot pie is perfect for a comforting dinner.

Serves 8 | Prep time 20 minutes | Cooking time 40 minutes

Ingredients

Crust
2 cups almond flour
1 egg
6 tablespoons unsalted butter, softened
¼ teaspoon salt
½ cup shredded cheddar cheese

Filling
2 tablespoons unsalted butter
½ cup onion, chopped
½ cup celery, chopped
1½ cups chicken broth
4 ounces cream cheese, softened
¼ cup heavy cream
¼ teaspoon poultry seasoning
1 teaspoon garlic powder
¼ teaspoon celery seed
Salt to taste
¼ teaspoon pepper
½ teaspoon xanthan gum
2 cups shredded rotisserie chicken
⅔ cup frozen carrots

Directions

1. Preheat the oven to 375°F.
2. Grease a 9-inch pie plate.
3. For the crust, add the flour, egg, butter, and salt to a large bowl and mix well with a mixer.
4. Add the cheese and stir to combine.
5. Divide the dough into 2 pieces and shape each into a ball.
6. Place each dough ball between two lightly greased sheets of parchment paper and roll into a circle to fit the pie plate.
7. Refrigerate the rolled dough inside the parchment paper for 5–10 minutes.
8. Place one sheet of dough on a smooth surface and carefully remove the parchment paper.
9. Place the dough in the prepared pie plate and press to fit.
10. Bake for 6–8 minutes.

11. Meanwhile, in a skillet, melt the butter over medium heat and sauté the onion and celery for about 5 minutes.
12. Add the chicken broth, cream cheese, and heavy cream and stir until smooth.
13. Add the poultry seasoning, garlic powder, celery seed, salt, and pepper, and stir to combine.
14. Reduce heat to low and stir in the xanthan gum until the mixture thickens.
15. Stir in the chicken and carrots and remove from heat.
16. Place the chicken mixture over the baked pie crust and arrange the remaining pie crust on top.
17. With your hands, press the top and bottom crusts together.
18. Bake for 25–30 minutes or until the crust is brown.
19. Remove from the oven and set aside for about 5 minutes before serving.

Nutrition (per serving)
Calories 470, fat 37.8 g, carbs 8 g, sugar 2.5 g,
Protein 17.5 g, sodium 813 mg

Chicken Marsala
(Cheesecake Factory)

An Italian-American dish of pan-fried chicken and mushrooms in a rich Marsala wine sauce. This one-pan chicken and mushroom dish is perfect for a busy weeknight.

Serves 4 | Prep time 15 minutes | Cooking time 30 minutes

Ingredients
4 (6-ounces) boneless, skinless chicken breast halves
Salt and pepper to taste
3 tablespoons olive oil (divided)
½ pound fresh baby Portobello mushrooms, sliced
2 cloves garlic, minced
1 cup Marsala wine
⅔ cup heavy whipping cream
½ cup Gorgonzola cheese, crumbled
2 tablespoons fresh parsley, minced

Directions
1. Season the chicken breasts with salt and pepper.
2. In a large wok, heat 2 tablespoons of oil over medium heat and cook the chicken for 6–8 minutes per side.
3. Transfer the chicken breasts to a plate and cover with foil to keep warm.
4. In the same wok, heat the remaining oil and sauté the mushrooms for 5–6 minutes.
5. Add the garlic and cook for about 1 minute.
6. Stir in the wine and bring to a boil, scraping up the browned bits from the bottom.
7. Cook for 1–2 minutes.
8. Stir in the cream and salt and again bring to a boil.
9. Cook for 2–3 minutes or until slightly thickened.
10. Stir in the cooked chicken and cheese and cook until the cheese is melted.
11. Serve hot topped with parsley.

Nutrition (per serving)
Calories 621, fat 36.7 g, carbs 5.9 g, sugar 1.4 g,
Protein 56.3 g, sodium 427 mg

Chicken Madeira
(Cheesecake Factory)

A combination of Madeira wine, mushrooms, beef broth, and mozzarella cheese. This Madeira sauce gives a depth of flavor to the chicken.

Serves 4 | Prep time 15 minutes | Cooking time 35 minutes

Ingredients
Chicken
4 boneless, skinless chicken breasts
Salt and pepper to taste
3 tablespoons olive oil
1 cup shredded mozzarella cheese

Sauce
2 tablespoons olive oil
½ pound fresh mushrooms, sliced
2 cups beef broth

3 cups Madeira wine
2 tablespoons arrowroot starch
2 tablespoons cold water
1 tablespoon butter
Pepper to taste

Directions
1. With a meat mallet, pound the chicken breasts to ¼ inch thick. Season with salt and pepper.
2. In a large wok, heat the olive oil over medium heat and cook the chicken breasts for 3–4 minutes per side.
3. Transfer the chicken breasts to a baking dish and cover them with foil to keep warm.
4. For the sauce, in the same wok, heat 2 tablespoons of oil over medium heat and cook the mushrooms for 1–2 minutes, stirring frequently.
5. Meanwhile, in a small bowl, dissolve the arrowroot starch in water.
6. Add the arrowroot starch mixture and the remaining sauce ingredients to the wok and stir to combine.
7. Increase heat to medium-high and bring to a boil.
8. Reduce heat to low and simmer for about 20 minutes.
9. Meanwhile, preheat the oven to broiler.
10. Sprinkle the chicken breasts with cheese and broil for 3–4 minutes.
11. Remove the baking dish from the oven and transfer the chicken breasts to serving plates.
12. Top with mushroom sauce and serve.

Nutrition (per serving)
Calories 595, fat 30.9 g, carbs 7.7 g, sugar 2.4 g,
Protein 39.3 g, sodium 554 mg

Chicken Limone
(Buca de Beppo)

A succulent chicken recipe that will become a favorite meal. The capers sauce with a touch of lemon and spices gives the chicken a wonderful flavor.

Serves 4 | Prep time 15 minutes | Cooking time 25 minutes

Ingredients
1 egg
3 tablespoons lemon juice (divided)
⅓ cup almond flour
⅛ teaspoon paprika
⅛ teaspoon garlic powder
4 (4-ounce) boneless, skinless chicken breasts, pounded
¼ cup butter
2 teaspoons chicken bouillon
½ cup hot water

1 tablespoon capers

Directions
1. In a shallow bowl, beat the egg with 1 tablespoon of lemon juice.
2. In another shallow bowl, mix the flour, paprika, and garlic powder.
3. Dip each chicken breast in the egg mixture and then coat it with the flour mixture.
4. In a large skillet, melt the butter over medium-high heat and cook the chicken breasts for 2–3 minutes per side.
5. Meanwhile, in a small bowl, dissolve the bouillon in the hot water.
6. Stir in the bouillon mixture and remaining lemon juice into the skillet and bring to a boil.
7. Reduce heat to low and simmer for 10–15 minutes.
8. Serve hot garnished with capers.

Nutrition (per serving)
Calories 397, fat 26.1 g, carbs 2.2 g, sugar 0.7 g,
Protein 34.5 g, sodium 274 mg

Chicken Picatta (Olive Garden)

One of the best family favorite chicken recipes, this chicken meal can be enjoyed any day of the week.

Serves 4 | Prep time 15 minutes | Cooking time 35 minutes

Ingredients
4 (6-ounce) boneless, skinless chicken breasts, pounded to ¼-inch thick
Salt and pepper to taste
3 tablespoons olive oil
1 small onion, chopped
10 sun-dried tomatoes, cut into strips
1 tablespoon minced garlic
¼ cup capers, drained and rinsed
1½ cups chicken broth
2 tablespoons lemon juice
3 tablespoons butter
⅓ cup heavy cream

Directions
1. Season the chicken breasts with salt and pepper.
2. In a skillet, heat the oil over medium-high heat and cook the chicken breasts for 5–8 minutes per side.
3. Transfer the chicken breasts to a plate.
4. In the same skillet, sauté the onion, sun-dried tomatoes, and garlic for 1–2 minutes.
5. Stir in the capers, broth, and lemon juice and scrape up the browned bits from the bottom of the skillet.
6. Reduce heat to medium-low and simmer for 10–15 minutes or until the desired thickness of the sauce.
7. Remove from heat and stir in the butter until melted completely.
8. Stir in the cream and return the skillet to medium-low heat.
9. Cook for about 1 minute, stirring continuously.
10. Stir in the cooked chicken breasts and remove from heat.
11. Serve immediately.

Nutrition (per serving)
Calories 554, fat 36.1 g, carbs 4 g, sugar 1.5 g,
Protein 52 g, sodium 756 mg

Chicken Parmigiana (Olive Garden)

A delectably flavorful chicken dish for dinner. This rich and flavorful chicken parmigiana will surely be a great choice for a dinner party.

Serves 4 | Prep time 15 minutes | Cooking time 20 minutes

Ingredients
Parmesan Mixture
1 cup grated Parmesan cheese
½ cup almond flour
2 teaspoons Italian seasoning
1 teaspoon garlic powder
1 teaspoon onion powder
Salt and pepper to taste

Egg Mixture
2 large eggs
½ teaspoon Italian seasoning
½ teaspoon garlic powder
Salt and pepper to taste

Chicken
1 pound chicken breasts
Salt and pepper to taste
2 tablespoons olive oil
1½ cups sugar-free marinara sauce
½ pound mozzarella cheese, sliced

Directions
1. Preheat the oven to 425°F. Arrange a rack in the middle.
2. In a shallow dish, mix together all of the Parmesan mixture ingredients.
3. In another shallow dish, beat all of the egg mixture ingredients.
4. Lightly coat each chicken breast with the Parmesan mixture, then dip into the egg mixture, and finally coat generously with the Parmesan mixture.
5. Season the chicken breasts with salt and pepper.
6. Heat the olive oil in a large nonstick wok over medium-high heat and cook the chicken breasts for 3–5 minutes per side.
7. Spread a layer of marinara sauce in the bottom of a baking dish.
8. Arrange the cooked chicken breasts on top of the marinara sauce.
9. Pour the remaining marinara sauce over the chicken breasts and top with cheese.
10. Bake for about 8–10 minutes or until the cheese is bubbly.

Nutrition (per serving)
Calories 571, fat 34.8 g, carbs 8.5 g, sugar 3.6 g,
Protein 52.6 g, sodium 861 mg

Mexican Grill Chicken (Chipotle)

A tasty and luscious chicken recipe with a great combo of spices which gives a perfect tasty flavoring to the chicken thighs.

Serves 8 | Prep time 15 minutes | Cooking time 10 minutes

Ingredients
1 ounce dried chipotle chili pepper
1 ounce dried ancho chili pepper
½ cup water
½ red onion, cut into small chunks
4 cloves garlic, peeled
1 teaspoon dried oregano
2 teaspoons salt
1 teaspoon ground cumin
1 teaspoon pepper
2 tablespoons olive oil

2½ pounds skinless, boneless chicken thighs, trimmed and pounded slightly

Directions
1. In a bowl, cover both chili peppers with water.
2. Cover and set aside for at least 10–12 hours.
3. Drain the water and remove the seeds from the peppers.
4. In a blender, pulse the chili peppers, onion, garlic, oregano, salt, cumin, and pepper until coarse paste forms.
5. Add the olive oil and pulse until smooth.
6. Place the chicken and paste it into a sealable plastic bag. Seal the bag and shake to coat well.
7. Marinate in the refrigerator for at least 8 hours.
8. Preheat a grill to medium-high heat. Grease the grate.
9. Remove the chicken from the bag and discard the marinade.
10. Grill the chicken for about 5 minutes per side or until desired doneness.
11. Place the chicken on a cutting board for about 5 minutes.
12. Cut into strips and serve.

Nutrition (per serving)
Calories 214, fat 8.7 g, carbs 1.6 g, sugar 0.3 g, Protein 31.9 g, sodium 520 mg

Crispy Fried Chicken (KFC)

Every kid's favorite recipe for fried chicken, this makes perfect fried chicken with the crispiest, most flavorful crunchy outside and moist inside.

Serves 8 | Prep time 10 minutes | Cooking time 20 minutes

Ingredients
1 egg white
1½ cups almond flour
1 tablespoon erythritol
½ teaspoon dried sage
½ teaspoon dried basil
½ teaspoon dried oregano
½ teaspoon dried marjoram
1 tablespoon paprika
1 teaspoon chili powder
1 teaspoon pepper
½ teaspoon ground allspice
1 tablespoon salt
2 teaspoons onion salt

½ teaspoon celery salt
½ teaspoon garlic powder
1 (3½–4 pound) whole chicken, cut into 8 pieces
6–8 cups olive oil

Directions
1. In a shallow bowl, slightly beat the egg white.
2. In another shallow bowl, mix together the flour, erythritol, dried herbs, and spices.
3. Dip each chicken breast in the beaten egg white and then coat with the flour mixture.
4. Set the chicken breasts aside for about 5 minutes.
5. In a deep fryer, heat the oil over medium heat. Fry the chicken breasts and wings for 12–14 minutes, flipping occasionally.
6. With a slotted spoon, transfer the chicken pieces onto a paper-towel-lined platter to drain.
7. Fry the chicken thighs and legs for 14–16 minutes, flipping occasionally.
8. With a slotted spoon, transfer the chicken pieces onto a paper-towel-lined platter to drain.
9. Serve hot.

Nutrition (per serving)
Calories 1500, fat 150.1 g, carbs 4.9 g, sugar 0.9 g,
Protein 49.9 g, sodium 913 mg

Instant Pot General Tso Chicken (Panda Express)

A sweet and spicy chicken dish the entire family will enjoy. This homemade chicken dish will fill your home with a fantastic aroma.

Serves 4 | Prep time 15 minutes | Cooking time 12 minutes

Ingredients
Sauce
3 cloves garlic, minced
½ teaspoon fresh ginger, minced
5 tablespoons low-sodium soy sauce
2 tablespoons sugar-free ketchup
1 teaspoon sesame oil
1 teaspoon chili paste
1 teaspoon erythritol

Chicken
1½ pounds boneless chicken thighs, cut into bite-sized pieces
¼ teaspoon salt
¼ teaspoon pepper
2 egg whites, beaten
½ cup almond flour
2 tablespoons coconut oil
½ cup chicken broth
½ teaspoon xanthan gum

Directions
1. In a bowl, beat all of the sauce ingredients until well combined.
2. Season the chicken pieces with salt and pepper.
3. Place the almond flour in a shallow dish.
4. Dip the chicken pieces in the egg and then coat with the flour.
5. Place the oil in the Instant Pot and select SAUTE. Add the chicken pieces and cook for 3–4 minutes.
6. Add the broth and scrape the brown bits from the bottom.
7. Select CANCEL and stir in the sauce.
8. Secure the lid and place the pressure valve in the SEAL position.
9. Select MANUAL and cook under high pressure for about 4 minutes.
10. Select CANCEL and carefully do a quick pressure release.
11. Remove the lid and select SAUTE.
12. Immediately stir in the xanthan gum and cook for 1–2 minutes or until the sauce thickens.
13. Select CANCEL and serve hot.

Nutrition (per serving)
Calories 566, fat 43.2 g, carbs 8 g, sugar 2.3 g, Protein 33 g, sodium 1400 mg

Chicken Tenders (Chick-fil-A)

A really delicious, healthy, and nutritious chicken recipe for all. These delicious chicken tenders are moist on the inside and crunchy on the outside.

Serves 8 | Prep time 15 minutes | Cooking time 6 minutes

Ingredients
Chicken
8 chicken tenders
Juice from a 24-ounce jar of dill pickles
¾ cup almond flour
1 teaspoon salt
1 teaspoon pepper
2 eggs
1½ cups pork rinds, crushed
Coconut oil

Sauce
½ cup mayonnaise
2 tablespoons Yacon syrup
1 tablespoon sugar-free BBQ sauce
2 teaspoons yellow mustard
1 teaspoon lemon juice

Directions
1. Place the chicken tenders and pickle juice in a large Ziploc bag. Seal the bag and shake to coat well.
2. Marinate in the refrigerator for at least 1 hour or overnight.
3. In a shallow bowl, mix together the almond flour, salt, and pepper.
4. In a second shallow bowl, lightly beat the egg.
5. In a third shallow bowl, place the pork rinds.
6. Coat the chicken tenders with the flour mixture, then dip into the beaten egg, and finally coat with pork rinds.
7. In a skillet, heat some coconut oil over medium-high heat and cook the chicken tenders for about 3 minutes per side or until golden brown.
8. With a slotted spoon, transfer the chicken tenders onto a paper towel-lined-plate to drain.
9. Mix all of the sauce ingredients together in a small bowl.

Nutrition (per serving)
Calories 917, fat 83.3 g, carbs 6.3 g, sugar 2.9 g, Protein 37.9 g, sodium 694 mg

KETO COPYCAT BEEF AND PORK RECIPES

Chili (Wendy's)

An authentic Mexican-style beef chili recipe that will win the heart of the pickiest eater.

Serves 8 | Prep time 15 minutes | Cooking time 1¾ hours

Ingredients
2 tablespoons olive oil
3 pounds ground beef
1 cup yellow onion, finely chopped
½ cup celery, finely chopped
½ cup green bell pepper, seeded and finely chopped

½ cup red bell pepper, seeded and finely chopped
1 (15-ounce) can crushed tomatoes with juice
1½ cups tomato juice
1½ teaspoons Worcestershire sauce
½ teaspoon dried oregano
2 teaspoons erythritol
3 tablespoons red chili powder
1 teaspoon ground cumin
1 teaspoon garlic powder
1 teaspoon salt
½ teaspoon pepper

Directions
1. In a large saucepan, heat the oil over medium-high heat and cook the beef for 8–10 minutes or until browned.
2. Drain the grease from the pan, leaving about 2 tablespoons inside.
3. Add the onions, celery, and bell peppers and cook over medium-high heat for about 5 minutes, stirring frequently.
4. Add the tomatoes, tomato juice, Worcestershire sauce, oregano, erythritol, and spices and stir to combine.
5. Reduce heat to low and simmer, covered, for 1–1½ hours, stirring occasionally.
6. Serve hot.

Nutrition (per serving)
Calories 372, fat 20.8 g, carbs 8 g, sugar 5 g,
Protein 36.3 g, sodium 574 mg

Mongolian Beef (P.F. Chang)

A restaurant-style dish that can easily be prepared at home. The combo of soy sauce, ginger, garlic, and red pepper flakes enhances the taste of flank steak in a great way.

Serves 4 | Prep time 15 minutes | Cooking time 16 minutes

Ingredients
3 tablespoons avocado oil (divided)
1 tablespoon minced garlic
2 teaspoons minced fresh ginger
¼ teaspoon red pepper flakes
¾ cup granulated erythritol
½ cup water
½ cup low-sodium soy sauce
1½ pounds flank steak, cut into ¼-inch-thick slices across the grain
¼ teaspoon xanthan gum
5 scallions, sliced thinly

Directions
1. For the sauce, heat 1 tablespoon of avocado oil in a medium saucepan over medium heat and sauté the ginger, garlic, and red pepper flakes for about 1 minute.
2. Stir in the erythritol, water, and soy sauce and bring to a boil.
3. Reduce heat to low and simmer for about 5 minutes or until thickened.
4. Transfer the sauce to a bowl and set aside.
5. For the steak, in a wok, heat the remaining avocado oil over medium-high heat and cook the beef slices for 2–3 minutes or until completely browned.
6. Add the sauce and xanthan gum and stir to combine.
7. Reduce heat to medium and cook for 2–3 minutes, stirring frequently.
8. Serve hot garnished with scallion.

Nutrition (per serving)
Calories 367, fat 15.6 g, carbs 5.6 g, sugar 2.5 g,
Protein 50 g, sodium 1620 mg

Beef and Broccoli (P.F. Chang)

When it comes to satisfying meals, beef and broccoli is at the top of the list. Slices of tender meat and broccoli with sauce will be on the dinner table in just 25 minutes.

Serves 4 | Prep time 15 minutes | Cooking time 8 minutes

Ingredients
Beef Marinade
2 tablespoons low-sodium soy sauce
1 tablespoon sesame oil
¼ teaspoon baking soda
1 pound sirloin steak, cut into ¼-inch-thick slices

Sauce
2 tablespoons low-sodium soy sauce
1 tablespoon Red Boat fish sauce
2½ teaspoons sesame oil

¼ teaspoon pepper
¼ teaspoon red pepper flakes, crushed

Cooking
1 head broccoli, cut into florets
2 tablespoons olive oil
2–3 cloves garlic, minced
1 teaspoon fresh ginger, finely chopped
½ teaspoon salt

Directions
1. For the marinade, add all of the marinade ingredients except for the beef slices to a large bowl and mix well.
2. Add the beef slices and coat generously with the marinade.
3. Set aside for about 15 minutes.
4. To make the sauce, add all of the sauce ingredients to a bowl and mix well. Set aside.
5. Place the broccoli and water in a microwave-safe bowl.
6. Cover and microwave for 2–3 minutes or until just tender.
7. In a skillet, heat the oil over medium-high heat and sauté the garlic, ginger, and salt for about 15 seconds.
8. Add the beef slices and stir to combine.
9. Increase the heat to high and cook for about 2 minutes per side.
10. Stir in the sauce and stir fry for about 1 minute.
11. Stir in the broccoli and stir fry for about 1 minute.
12. Serve hot.

Nutrition (per serving)
Calories 366, fat 21.3 g, carbs 6.2 g, sugar 2.1 g,
Protein 38.4 g, sodium 1400 mg

Beef Barbacoa (Chipotle)

A versatile and protein-rich dish for the dining table. Chipotle chilies, adobo sauce, lime juice, and vinegar accompany the chuck roast in a great way.

Serves 10 | Prep time 15 minutes | Cooking time 8 hours

Ingredients
½ cup beef broth
2 medium chipotle chilies in adobo
4 teaspoons adobo sauce (from the can of chilies)
5 cloves garlic, minced
2 tablespoons apple cider vinegar
2 tablespoons lime juice
1 tablespoon dried oregano
2 teaspoons ground cumin
2 teaspoons salt
1 teaspoon pepper
3 pounds chuck roast, trimmed and cut into 2-inch chunks

2 whole bay leaves

Directions
1. In a blender, pulse all of the ingredients except for the beef and bay leaves until smooth.
2. Place the beef chunks in a slow cooker.
3. Place the bay leaves over the beef chunks and top with the broth mixture.
4. Cook on LOW, covered, for 8–10 hours.
5. Discard the bay leaves. Shred the meat with two forks and stir it back into the pan sauce.
6. Cover the slow cooker for 5–10 minutes before serving.

Nutrition (per serving)
Calories 305, fat 11.5 g, carbs 2.1 g, sugar 0.6 g,
Protein 45.4 g, sodium 658 mg

Steak Fajita (Chili's)

A mouthwatering dish that is loaded with healthy nutrients and rich flavors. This mouthwatering dish will surely be a hit entree for weeknight dinner parties.

Serves 4 | Prep time 15 minutes | Cooking time 8 hours

Ingredients
1½ pounds sirloin steak, cut into bite-size pieces
1 (4-ounce) can diced green chilies
1 (1½-ounce) envelope dry onion soup mix
1 tablespoon lime juice
2 cups water
1 onion, cut into strips
1 red bell pepper, seeded and cut into strips
1 green bell pepper, seeded and cut into strips

Directions
1. Grease the pot of a slow cooker. Add the steak, chilies, soup mix, lime juice, and water and stir to combine.
2. Set the slow cooker on LOW and cook, covered, for 6–8 hours.

3. Heat some oil in a large skillet over medium-high heat and sauté the onion and bell peppers for 4–5 minutes.
4. Remove from heat and set aside.
5. With a slotted spoon, transfer the steak to a plate.
6. Add the bell pepper mixture and stir to combine.
7. Serve hot.

Nutrition (per serving)
Calories 352, fat 10.7 g, carbs 8.2 g, sugar 4.1 g, Protein 52.3 g, sodium 457 mg

Steak Diane
(Cheesecake Factory)

An astonishingly good recipe for pan-cooked beef medallions flavored with a creamy mushroom sauce.

Serves 2 | Prep time 15 minutes | Cooking time 15 minutes

Ingredients
¾ pound beef tenderloin, cut into 4 (3-ounce) medallions
Salt to taste
2 teaspoons cracked black peppercorns
2 tablespoons butter
½ cup fresh mushrooms, sliced
3 tablespoons pearl onions, chopped
¼ cup white wine
1 tablespoon Dijon mustard
1 teaspoon Worcestershire sauce
¾ cup beef broth
¼ cup cream

Directions
1. Season the beef with salt and pepper.
2. In a large, heavy skillet, melt 1 tablespoon of butter over medium heat and sear the beef medallions for 2–3 minutes per side or until desired doneness.
3. Transfer the beef medallions to a plate and cover them with foil.
4. In the same skillet, melt the remaining butter and cook the pearl onions for about 2 minutes.
5. Add the mushrooms and sauté for 1–2 minutes.
6. Add the wine and Worcestershire sauce and bring to a boil.
7. Stir in the mustard and cook for about 1 minute.
8. Stir in the broth and cook for about 1 minute.
9. Stir in the cream and bring to a boil.
10. Immediately remove from heat and stir in the chives.
11. Pour the mushroom sauce over the beef medallions and serve.

Nutrition (per serving)
Calories 528, fat 29.6 g, carbs 5 g, sugar 2.6 g,
Protein 52.5 g, sodium 675 mg

Meatloaf
(Cheesecake Factory)

A flavorful baked feast for gatherings of family and friends. Everyone will love to enjoy the wonderful flavors of this meatloaf.

Serves 6 | Prep time 15 minutes | Cooking time 50 minutes

Ingredients
1 pound lean ground beef
½ pound ground veal
½ pound ground pork
¾ cup large-curd cottage cheese
½ cup cheddar cheese, shredded
1 cup chopped onion
½ cup chopped scallion
½ cup crushed pork rinds
2 eggs
⅓ cup tomato sauce
¼ cup dry red wine
1 tablespoon Dijon mustard

Salt and pepper to taste

Directions
1. Preheat the oven to 350°F.
2. Lightly grease a 9×5-inch loaf pan.
3. In a large bowl, mix together all of the ingredients with your hands.
4. Place the mixture in the prepared loaf pan and use the back of a spoon to smooth the top surface.
5. Bake for about 50 minutes.
6. Remove the loaf pan from the oven and place on a wire rack to cool for about 10 minutes before serving.

Nutrition (per serving)
Calories 382, fat 15.1 g, carbs 4.8 g, sugar 1.9 g, Protein 52.4 g, sodium 475 mg

Mexican Grill Pork Carnitas (Chipotle)

A recipe for pulled pork with a delicious herb touch. This easy pulled-pork recipe cooked in the slow cooker makes the best pulled pork.

Serves 10 | Prep time 15 minutes | Cooking time 13 hours 8 minutes

Ingredients
5 pounds pork shoulder
2 tablespoons olive oil
2 teaspoons salt (divided)
2 teaspoons pepper (divided)
4 dried bay leaves
½ cup water
1 tablespoon dried rosemary
½ teaspoon dried thyme, crushed
Directions

1. Rinse the pork shoulder thoroughly under cold running water. Pat dry with paper towels.
2. Season with 1 teaspoon of salt and 1 teaspoon of pepper.
3. In a Dutch oven, heat the olive oil over medium-high heat and sear the pork shoulder for 3–4 minutes per side or until browned on all sides.
4. Remove the pork shoulder from the Dutch oven and set it aside.
5. In the Dutch oven, bring the water to a boil over medium-high heat, scraping the browned bits from the bottom with a wooden spoon.
6. Add the bay leaves to the bottom of the slow cooker. Top with the pork, followed by the liquid from the Dutch oven.
7. Sprinkle with herbs and the remaining salt and pepper. Stir well.
8. Set the slow cooker on LOW and cook, covered, for 10–12 hours.
9. Shred the meat with two forks.
10. Mix the shredded meat with the pan sauce.
11. Set the slow cooker on HIGH and cook, covered, for 30–60 minutes.
12. Serve hot.

Nutrition (per serving)
Calories 689, fat 51.4 g, carbs 0.5 g, sugar 0 g,
Protein 52.9 g, sodium 620 mg

Grilled Pork Chop (Cheesecake Factory)

A hit recipe for pork chops for the family and friends at your dinner table. These fabulous pork chops are so delicious.

Serves 4 | Prep time 15 minutes | Cooking time 15 minutes

Ingredients
2 cups cold water
¼ cup erythritol
¼ cup salt
2 cups ice water
4 (8-ounce, 1-inch-thick) center-cut pork rib chops
3 tablespoons paprika
½ teaspoon ground chipotle pepper
1 teaspoon garlic powder
1 teaspoon onion powder
1 teaspoon ground cumin
1 teaspoon ground mustard
Pepper to taste

2 tablespoons olive oil

Directions
1. Add the cold water to a large saucepan. Dissolve the erythritol and salt over medium heat.
2. Remove from heat and add the ice water. Set aside at room temperature to cool.
3. Add the brine and pork chops to a large resealable plastic bag. Seal the bag and press to coat the chops.
4. Place the bag in a 13×9-inch baking dish and refrigerate for 8–12 hours.
5. Remove the chops from the brine and rinse under cold running water. Pat them dry with paper towels.
6. In a small bowl, mix together the spices.
7. Brush the chops with oil and then coat with the spice mixture.
8. Set aside at room temperature for about 30 minutes.
9. Preheat the grill to medium heat. Grease the grate.
10. Grill the pork chops for 4–6 minutes per side or until desired doneness.
11. Remove from grill and set aside for about 5 minutes before serving.

Nutrition (per serving)
Calories 416, fat 24.7 g, carbs 4.9 g, sugar 1 g,
Protein 43.9 g, sodium 5000 mg

Baby Back Ribs (Outback Steakhouse)

One of the best and most delicious ways to prepare pork ribs. The seasoning rub and sauce complement the flavor of the pork ribs in a wonderful way.

Serves 4 | Prep time 15 minutes | Cooking time 10 minutes

Ingredients
Pork Ribs
4–5 pounds baby back ribs
1 (32-ounce) bottle sugar-free cola

Rub
2 teaspoons salt
1 teaspoon pepper
1 teaspoon garlic salt
½ teaspoon onion powder

½ teaspoon dried oregano

Sauce
½ cup sugar-free ketchup
3 tablespoons erythritol
1 tablespoon apple cider vinegar
½ tablespoon Worcestershire sauce
½ tablespoon liquid smoke
½ teaspoon garlic powder
½ teaspoon salt
¼–½ teaspoon chipotle powder

Directions
1. Place the ribs and cola in a large resealable bag. Seal the bag and shake to coat.
2. Refrigerate for at least 8 hours or overnight.
3. Preheat the oven to 350°F.
4. Mix all of the rub ingredients together in a bowl.
5. Drain the ribs, discarding the cola, and pat them dry with paper towels.
6. Rub the ribs with the spice mixture. Wrap them in foil.
7. Arrange the ribs on a baking sheet and bake for about 1 hour.
8. In a bowl, beat all of the sauce ingredients until well combined.
9. Preheat the grill to medium heat. Grease the grate.
10. Remove the ribs from the oven and set aside for about 5 minutes.
11. Carefully remove the foil from the ribs and then coat them with sauce.
12. Place the ribs on the grill and cook for about 15 minutes, occasionally flipping and brushing with the sauce.
13. Serve hot.

Nutrition (per serving)
Calories 1040, fat 55.5 g, carbs 7.6 g, sugar .70 g,
Protein 119.7 g, sodium 857 mg

KETO COPYCAT FISH AND SEAFOOD RECIPES

Fresh Grilled Salmon (Cheesecake Factory)

A super-fast and easy recipe for a healthy fish. This salmon is seasoned deliciously with a few ingredients.

Serves 6 | Prep time 10 minutes | Cooking time 10 minutes

Ingredients
⅓ cup olive oil
3 tablespoons low-sodium soy sauce
2 tablespoons Dijon mustard
½ teaspoon dried minced garlic
6 (5-ounce) salmon fillets

Directions
1. In a small bowl, mix the oil, soy sauce, mustard, and garlic.
2. Place the salmon fillets and half of the marinade in a large resealable plastic bag. Reserve the remaining marinade.
3. Seal the bag and shake to coat. Refrigerate for about 30 minutes.
4. Preheat the grill to medium-low heat. Grease the grate.
5. Remove the salmon fillets from the bag and discard the used marinade.
6. Place the salmon fillets on the grill and cook, covered, for 5–10 minutes or until desired doneness.
7. Transfer the salmon fillets to a serving platter and drizzle with the reserved marinade.
8. Serve immediately.

Nutrition (per serving)
Calories 290, fat 20.2 g, carbs 0.9 g, sugar 0.5 g, Protein 28.2 g, sodium 562 mg

Herb Crusted Salmon (Cheesecake Factory)

Omega-3 rich and super delicious salmon in a balanced, creamy sauce. Lemon pepper seasoning and fresh herbs balance the rich taste of salmon.

Serves 4 | Prep time 15 minutes | Cooking time 13 minutes

Ingredients
¾ teaspoon lemon pepper seasoning
1 teaspoon dried thyme
1 teaspoon dried parsley
4 (5-ounce) salmon fillets
5 tablespoons lemon juice (divided)
10 tablespoons butter (divided)
1 shallot, minced
5 tablespoons white wine (divided)
1 tablespoon white wine vinegar
1 cup half-and-half
Salt and ground white pepper to taste

Directions
1. In a small bowl, mix together the lemon pepper seasoning and dried herbs.
2. In a shallow dish, rub the salmon fillets with 3 tablespoons of lemon juice.
3. Season the non-skin side with the herb mixture. Set aside.
4. In a skillet, melt 2 tablespoons of butter over medium heat and sauté the shallot for about 2 minutes.
5. Stir in the remaining lemon juice, ¼ cup of wine, and the vinegar and simmer for 2–3 minutes.
6. Stir in the half-and-half, salt, and white pepper, and cook for 2–3 minutes.
7. Add ¼ cup of butter and stir until well combined.
8. Remove from heat and set aside, covered.
9. In a wok, melt the remaining butter over medium heat.
10. Place the salmon in the wok, herb side down, and cook for 1–2 minutes.
11. Transfer the salmon fillets to a plate, herb side up.
12. Add the remaining wine to the wok and scrape up the browned bits from the bottom.
13. Return the salmon fillets to the wok, herb side up, and cook for about 8 minutes.
14. Transfer the salmon fillets onto serving plates.
15. Top with the pan sauce and serve.

Nutrition (per serving)
Calories 546, fat 44.7 g, carbs 4.7 g, sugar 0.7 g,
Protein 29.9 g, sodium 337 mg

Pan-Fried Tilapia with Chimichurri Sauce (Bonefish Grill)

A family feast recipe for pan-seared tilapia with refreshing chimichurri sauce. Chimichurri sauce accompanies tilapia fillets nicely.

Serves 4 | Prep time 15 minutes | Cooking time 8 minutes

Ingredients
Tilapia
4 tilapia fillets
2 tablespoons BBQ seasoning
Salt and pepper to taste
2 teaspoons olive oil

Chimichurri Sauce
8 cloves garlic, minced

Salt to taste
1 teaspoon dried oregano
1 teaspoon pepper
1 teaspoon red pepper flakes, crushed
4–5 teaspoons lemon zest, finely grated
¼ cup lemon juice
1 bunch fresh flat-leaf parsley
1 cup olive oil

Directions
1. Add all of the chimichurri sauce ingredients to a food processor and pulse until well combined.
2. Transfer the sauce to a bowl and refrigerate for 30 minutes before serving.
3. Meanwhile, season the tilapia fillets with BBQ seasoning, salt, and pepper.
4. In a nonstick pan, heat the oil over medium-high heat and cook the tilapia fillets for 3–4 minutes per side or until cooked through.
5. Transfer the tilapia fillets to serving plates.
6. Top each fillet with chimichurri sauce and serve.

Nutrition (per serving)
Calories 575, fat 52.1 g, carbs 4.4 g, sugar 0.9 g,
Protein 27.2 g, sodium 237 mg

Parmesan Crusted Tilapia (Olive Garden)

Tilapia is broiled with a coating of Parmesan cheese, mayonnaise, and butter for an impressive meal. Seasoning adds a delish touch to the creamy and cheesy coating.

Serves 4 | Prep time 10 minutes | Cooking time 5 minutes

Ingredients
½ cup Parmesan cheese, grated
3 tablespoons butter, softened
2 tablespoons mayonnaise
¼ teaspoon dried basil
⅛ teaspoon celery salt
⅛ teaspoon onion powder
¼ teaspoon pepper
4 (6-ounce) tilapia fillets
4 lemon wedges
Directions

1. Preheat the oven to broiler. Arrange the oven rack about 4 inches from the heating element.
2. Grease a baking dish.
3. In a small bowl, mix all of the ingredients except for the tilapia fillets and lemon wedges.
4. Arrange the fillets in the prepared baking dish in a single layer.
5. Sprinkle the cheese mixture over the fillets.
6. Broil for 4–5 minutes or until the topping is lightly browned, rotating the baking dish once halfway through.
7. Serve hot with lemon wedges.

Nutrition (per serving)
Calories 282, fat 15 g, carbs 1.9 g, sugar 0.5 g, Protein35.8 g, sodium 260 mg

Tilapia Picatta (Olive Garden)

A fantastic dinner that is prepared within 25 minutes. The lemony caper sauce makes the tilapia flavorful.

Serves 4 | Prep time 15 minutes | Cooking time 8 minutes

Ingredients
3 tablespoons lemon juice
2 tablespoons olive oil
2 cloves garlic, minced
½ teaspoon lemon zest, grated
2 teaspoons capers, drained
3 tablespoons fresh basil, minced (divided)
4 (6-ounce) tilapia fillets
Salt and pepper

Directions
1. Preheat oven to broiler. Arrange an oven rack about 4 inches from the heating element.
2. In a small bowl, beat the lemon juice, oil, garlic, and lemon zest until well combined.
3. Add the capers and 2 tablespoons of basil and stir to combine.
4. Reserve 2 tablespoons of the mixture in a small bowl.
5. Coat the fish fillets with the remaining capers mixture and sprinkle with salt and pepper.
6. Place the tilapia fillets on a greased broiler pan and broil for 3–4 minutes per side.
7. Remove from the oven and place the fish fillets on serving plates.
8. Drizzle with the reserved capers mixture and serve garnished with remaining basil.

Nutrition (per serving)
Calories 206, fat 8.7 g, carbs 0.9 g, sugar 0.3 g,
Protein 31.9 g, sodium 144 mg

Shrimp Orleans (Chris Ruth Steakhouse)

A restaurant-quality dinner dish that is super-quick to prepare with a wonderful taste. Pan-seared shrimp and rich wine sauce marry each other nicely.

Serves 4 | Prep time 15 minutes | Cooking time 10 minutes

Ingredients
2 cups butter, softened
¼ cup garlic, chopped
½ teaspoon dried rosemary, crushed
2 teaspoons Worcestershire sauce
1 teaspoon Tabasco sauce
2 teaspoons pepper
1½ teaspoons paprika
¼ teaspoon cayenne pepper
1 teaspoon salt
1½ teaspoons water
1 tablespoon + 1 teaspoon olive oil

1 pound shrimp, peeled and deveined
¼ cup scallions, chopped
½ cup dry white wine

Directions
1. Add the butter, garlic, rosemary, Worcestershire sauce, Tabasco sauce, black pepper, paprika, cayenne pepper, salt, and water to a bowl.
2. Beat with an electric mixer on high speed until well combined. Refrigerate until ready to serve.
3. In a large saucepan, heat the oil over medium-high heat and cook the shrimp for 1–2 minutes.
4. Reduce heat to medium and flip the shrimp.
5. Add the scallions and cook for 1–2 minutes.
6. Add the white wine and cook until reduced to ¼ cup.
7. Add 1 cup of the butter mixture and stir to combine.
8. Reduce heat to low and cook for 1–2 minutes, stirring frequently.
9. Remove from heat and transfer to a warm bowl.
10. Serve immediately.

Nutrition (per serving)
Calories 1025, fat 97.6 g, carbs 7 g, sugar 1.1 g,
Protein 27.7 g, sodium 1139 mg

Shrimp Scampi (Red Lobster)

A wonderfully delicious shrimp supper that is really easy to cook. Shrimp are simmered in a delish sauce of butter, lemon, and herbs for a nice meal.

Serves 4 | Prep time 15 minutes | Cooking time 15 minutes

Ingredients
1 pound medium shrimp, peeled and deveined
Salt and pepper to taste
1 tablespoon olive oil
3 cloves garlic, minced
1½ cups white wine
2 tablespoons lemon juice
¼ teaspoon dried thyme
¼ teaspoon dried rosemary
¼ teaspoon dried oregano
¼ teaspoon dried basil
½ cup unsalted butter, softened
2 tablespoons fresh parsley, chopped
¼ cup grated Parmesan cheese

Directions
1. Season the shrimp with salt and pepper.
2. Heat the olive oil in a large cast-iron skillet over medium-high heat and cook the shrimp for 2–3 minutes, stirring occasionally.
3. With a slotted spoon, transfer the shrimp to a plate and set aside.
4. In the same skillet, sauté the garlic for about 1 minute.
5. Stir in the white wine and lemon juice and bring to a boil.
6. Reduce heat to low and simmer for 4–5 minutes.
7. Add the dried herbs and stir to combine.
8. Slowly add the butter and stir until melted and smooth.
9. Sir in the cooked shrimp, parsley, salt, and pepper and remove from heat.
10. Serve immediately garnished with Parmesan.

Nutrition (per serving)
Calories 353, fat 23.2 g, carbs 2.9 g, sugar 0.7 g,
Protein 21.5 g, sodium 348 mg

Cajun Shrimp (Red Lobster)

A one-pan supper that is really tasty and healthy. The combo of mustard, herbs, and spices gives a really aromatic and flavorsome touch to the shrimp.

Serves 4 | Prep time 15 minutes | Cooking time 20 minutes

Ingredients
½ cup butter
1 pound medium shrimp, peeled and deveined
2¼ teaspoon dry mustard
1 teaspoon dried thyme
1 teaspoon dried oregano
4 teaspoons cayenne pepper
3 teaspoons salt
2 teaspoons pepper
2 teaspoons paprika
2 teaspoons ground cumin

2 teaspoons garlic powder
2 teaspoons onion powder

Directions
1. Preheat the oven to 400°F.
2. Place the butter in a 13×9-inch baking dish and then place the pan in the oven while preheating.
3. In a small bowl, mix together the mustard, dried herbs, and spices.
4. Remove the baking dish from the oven.
5. Add the shrimp and spice mixture and mix well with the melted butter. Arrange the shrimp in a single layer.
6. Bake for about 15 minutes.
7. Serve hot.

Nutrition (per serving)
Calories 373, fat 27.8 g, carbs 6 g, sugar 0.8 g,
Protein 27.4 g, sodium 877 mg

Mussels di Napoli
(Olive Garden)

With just simple ingredients, this recipe makes the perfect light meal for all. Mussels are cooked in a buttery wine sauce to make an elegant meal for a dinner party.

Serves 4 | Prep time 15 minutes | Cooking time 9 minutes

Ingredients
2 tablespoons olive oil
5 cloves garlic, chopped
2 pounds mussels, cleaned and debearded
1 cup white wine
½ cup salted butter
1 tablespoon parsley, minced
1 tablespoon Italian seasoning
⅛ teaspoon red pepper flakes, crushed
¼ teaspoon salt
¼ teaspoon pepper

Directions
1. In a nonstick pan, heat the oil over medium heat and sauté the garlic for about 1 minute. Remove from heat.
2. To a large pan over medium heat, add the mussels, wine, butter, and garlic oil.
3. Cover and bring to a boil.
4. Cook for 1–2 minutes.
5. Discard any unopened mussels.
6. Add the remaining ingredients and stir gently to combine.
7. Reduce heat to low and simmer for about 2 minutes.
8. Serve hot.

Nutrition (per serving)
Calories 459 fat 35.1 g, carbs 7 g, sugar 0 g,
Protein 27.3 g, sodium 960 mg

Crab Cakes (Red Lobster)

A really delicious way to prepare crab cakes. This combination of mustard, mayonnaise, egg, and seasoning gives a tasty richness to crab meat.

Serves 8 | Prep time 15 minutes | Cooking time 14 minutes

Ingredients
1 tablespoon onion, minced
1 tablespoon celery, finely chopped
½ teaspoon garlic, minced
1 egg
2 tablespoons mayonnaise
1 teaspoon Dijon mustard
1 teaspoon Old Bay seasoning
⅛ teaspoon salt
⅛ teaspoon pepper
1 pound lump crab meat
½ cup pork rinds, crushed (divided)
2 tablespoons olive oil

Directions
1. In a large bowl, mix together all of the ingredients except for the crab meat, pork rinds, and oil.
2. Add the crab meat and stir gently to combine.
3. Add ¼ cup of pork rinds and stir gently to combine.
4. Make balls from the mixture.
5. Place the remaining pork rinds in a shallow bowl.
6. Gently flatten each ball into a patty. Coat with the pork rinds.
7. In a large skillet, heat the oil over medium heat and cook the patties for 2–3 minutes per side.
8. Reduce heat to low and cook for 5–8 minutes.
9. Serve hot.

Nutrition (per serving)
Calories 106, fat 10.6 g, carbs 2.1 g, sugar 0.4 g,
Protein 10.2 g, sodium 513mg

KETO COPYCAT DESSERT RECIPES

Chocolate Frosty (Wendy's)

A decadent homemade chocolate frosty recipe that gets its rich flavor from cacao powder and vanilla.

Serves 2-4 | Prep time 10 minutes | Chill time 60 minutes

Ingredients
1 cup heavy whipping cream
1 tablespoon almond butter
2 tablespoons cacao powder
½ teaspoon liquid stevia
1 teaspoon vanilla extract
Fruit slice for garnish (optional)

Directions
1. In the bowl of a stand mixer, beat all of the ingredients until stiff peaks form.
2. Freeze the mixture for 40–60 minutes until barely frozen.
3. Place the frosty in a plastic freezer bag or piping bag fitted with a large tip.
4. Cut one corner of the plastic bag to pipe into serving cups.
5. Garnish with sliced fruits if desired and serve immediately.

Nutrition (per serving)
Calories 137, fat 13.9 g, carbs 3 g, sugar 0.3 g,
Protein 2 g, sodium 12 mg

Zabaglione (Olive Garden)

A delicious dessert bowl of fresh strawberries with a wine-flavored custard topping. This custard is prepared with egg yolks, wine, and erythritol.

Serves 2 | Prep time 10 minutes | Cooking time 20 minutes

Ingredients
½ cup fresh strawberries, hulled and sliced
3 tablespoons + 1 teaspoon erythritol (divided)
¼ cup dry Marsala wine
3 large egg yolks

Directions
1. In a bowl, gently toss the strawberries with 1 teaspoon of erythritol to coat.
2. Cover and set aside at room temperature for about 1 hour.

3. Divide the strawberries into 2 small serving bowls.
4. In a small pan, add the wine, egg yolk, and remaining erythritol over low heat and cook for 7–8 minutes, beating continuously.
5. Remove from heat and pour the custard over the strawberries.
6. Serve warm.

Nutrition (per serving)
Calories 117, fat 6.9 g, carbs 4.5 g, sugar 2.1 g,
Protein 4.3 g, sodium 14 mg

Glazed Doughnuts (Krispy Kreme)

The best way to prepare delicious vanilla-flavored doughnuts. These delicious doughnuts will be a hit when your kid demands a yummy dessert.

Serves 6 | Prep time 15 minutes | Cooking time 16 minutes

Ingredients
Doughnuts
2 eggs
½ cup almond flour
¼ cup unsweetened protein powder
2 tablespoons coconut flour
¼ cup erythritol
¼ teaspoon salt
2 teaspoons baking powder
1 teaspoon vanilla extract
⅛–¼ cup unsweetened vanilla almond milk

Glaze
¼ cup butter, melted
¼ cup erythritol
1 teaspoon vanilla extract

Directions
1. Preheat the oven to 350°F.
2. Grease a doughnut pan.
3. In a bowl, mix together all of the doughnut ingredients.
4. Fill each prepared doughnut hole about ¾ full with the mixture.
5. Bake for about 14–16 minutes or until the top becomes golden brown.
6. Remove from the oven and place the pan on a wire rack to cool completely.
7. In a bowl, beat all of the glaze ingredients until well combined.
8. Spread the glaze over the doughnuts and serve.

Nutrition (per serving)
Calories 193, fat 15.1 g, carbs 5.4 g, sugar 0.9 g,
Protein 6.9 g, sodium 231 mg

Cranberry Bliss Bars (Starbucks)

A lush and super-tasty recipe that delivers a classic dessert. This cookie bar is prepared with white chocolate chips and dried cranberries.

Serves 12 | Prep time 20 minutes | Cooking time 32 minutes

Ingredients
Cookie layer
2 cups almond flour
½ cup powdered erythritol
1 teaspoon baking powder
Pinch of salt
½ cup butter, softened
1 egg
1 teaspoon vanilla extract
⅓ cup dried unsweetened cranberries, chopped
4 ounces sugar-free white chocolate chips

Icing
6 ounces cream cheese, softened
½ cup powdered erythritol
½ teaspoon vanilla extract
½ teaspoon almond extract
2 tablespoons dried unsweetened cranberries, chopped
¼ cup sugar-free white chocolate chips
1 tablespoon coconut oil

Directions
1. Preheat the oven to 325°F.
2. Grease a 9×9-inch baking dish.
3. Add all of the cookie layer ingredients, except for the cranberries and chocolate chips, to a bowl. With an electric mixer, blend on high speed until smooth and creamy.
4. Add the cranberries and chocolate chips and stir gently to combine.
5. Place the mixture in the baking dish and spread it evenly with a spatula.
6. Bake for 25–30 minutes or until browned.
7. Remove the baking dish from the oven and place it on a wire rack to cool completely.
8. To make the icing, in a bowl, beat the cream cheese, erythritol, and both extracts until creamy and fluffy.
9. Spread the icing over the cookie layer and sprinkle with cranberries.
10. In a microwave-safe bowl, microwave the chocolate chips and coconut oil on high for 1½–2 minutes or until melted completely, stirring every 15 seconds.
11. Remove from the microwave and stir until smooth.
12. Cut the cookie layer into desired-sized pieces and drizzle with melted chocolate.
13. Refrigerate until completely set before serving.

Nutrition (per serving)
Calories 321, fat 27.2 g, carbs 10 g, sugar 7 g,
Protein 2.3 g, sodium 124 mg

Original Cheesecake (Cheesecake Factory)

An incredibly luscious and yummy cheesecake dessert. This light and fluffy cheesecake is packed with the flavors of cream cheese, sour cream, and lemon.

Serves 16 | Prep time 20 minutes | Cooking time 1¼ hours

Ingredients
Crust
¾ cup almond meal
¼ cup walnuts, finely ground
¼ cup pecans, finely ground
¼ cup almonds, finely ground
2 tablespoons butter, melted

Filling
1½ pounds cream cheese, softened
1⅓ cups granulated erythritol
5 eggs

¼ cup unflavored whey protein isolate
2 teaspoons vanilla extract
2 teaspoons lemon juice
1 pound sour cream

Directions
1. Preheat the oven to 325°F.
2. In a bowl, mix all of the crust ingredients until a crumbly mixture forms.
3. Add the crust mixture to a 9-inch springform pan and press to cover the bottom and 1½ inches up the sides.
4. For the filling, in the bowl of a stand mixer, beat the cream cheese on low speed until light and fluffy.
5. Add the erythritol a little at a time and beat continuously until creamy.
6. Add the eggs one at a time, beating well after each addition.
7. Add the protein powder, vanilla, and lemon juice and mix until just combined.
8. Add the sour cream and beat until just combined.
9. Place the cream cheese mixture over the crust in the springform pan and smooth the surface with a spoon.
10. Bake for 1–1¼ hours or until the cheesecake jiggles slightly in the middle when the pan is gently shaken.
11. Turn the oven off and prop the oven door open.
12. Let the cheesecake stay in the oven for about 1 hour.
13. Remove the springform pan from the oven and place on a wire rack to cool.
14. Refrigerate for about 24 hours before serving.

Nutrition (per serving)
Calories 310, fat 29.2 g, carbs 4.4 g, sugar 0.8 g,
Protein 9.2 g, sodium 173 mg

Pumpkin Cheesecake (Cheesecake Factory)

A luscious and richly flavored cheesecake recipe for a holiday dessert table. Warm spices and vanilla give a delish flavoring to the pumpkin.

Serves 12 | Prep time 20 minutes | Cooking time 1½ hours

Ingredients
Crust
½ cup pecans
2 cups almond flour
⅓ cup butter, melted
1 tablespoon erythritol
1 teaspoon vanilla extract

Filling
4 (8-ounce) packages cream cheese, softened
¼ cup sour cream

4 teaspoons ground cinnamon
1 teaspoon ground ginger
¼ teaspoon ground cloves
¼ teaspoon ground nutmeg
1 (15-ounce) can pure pumpkin
2¾ cups powdered erythritol
1 tablespoon vanilla extract
4 large eggs, lightly beaten

Directions
1. Preheat the oven to 325°F.
2. For the crust, in a food processor, pulse the pecans into small pieces.
3. Add the remaining ingredients and pulse until a crumbly mixture forms.
4. Add the crust mixture to a 9-inch springform pan and press to cover the bottom and 1½ inches up the sides.
5. Bake for about 10–15 minutes.
6. Remove from the oven set aside to cool. Leave the oven set at 325°F.
7. For the filling, in a bowl, beat the cream cheese until smooth.
8. Mix in the sour cream.
9. Add the remaining ingredients except for the eggs and beat until well combined.
10. Add the eggs and mix until just combined.
11. Place the filling mixture over the crust in the springform pan and smooth the surface with a spoon.
12. Bake for 1–1¼ hours or until the cheesecake jiggles slightly in the middle when the pan is gently shaken.
13. Turn the oven off and prop the oven door open.
14. Let the cheesecake stay in the oven for about 1 hour.
15. Remove the springform pan from the oven and place on a wire rack to cool.
16. Refrigerate for about 24 hours before serving.

Nutrition (per serving)
Calories 517, fat 48 g, carbs 9.1 g, sugar 2,5 g,
Protein 9 g, sodium 288 mg

Lemon Pound Cake (Starbucks)

Prepare a delightfully great and refreshingly tasty cake for your family. You will surely receive huge appreciation from all.

Serves 10 | Prep time 15 minutes
Cooking time 45 minutes

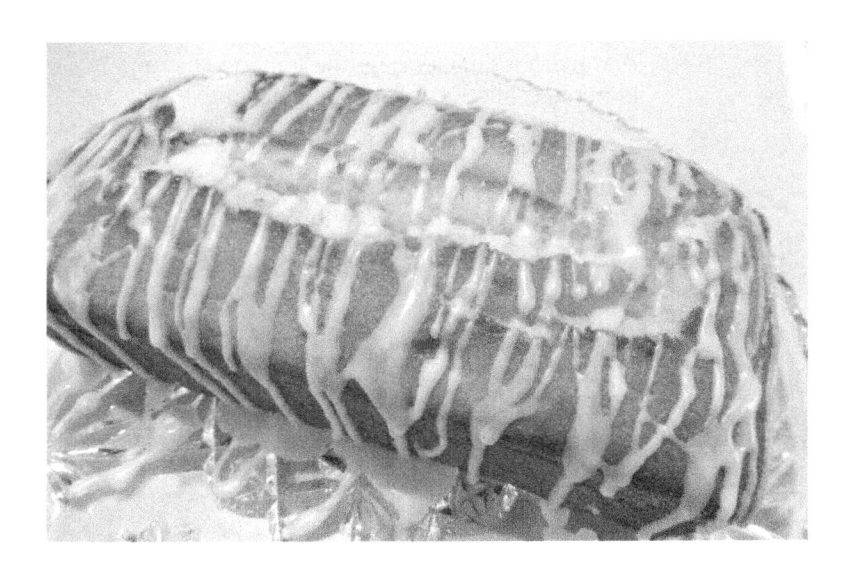

Ingredients
Cake
2 cups almond flour
¼ cup coconut flour
1 tablespoon baking powder
5 eggs
¾ cup monk fruit sweetener
½ cup butter, melted
¼ cup lemon juice
1 tablespoon lemon extract

Frosting
½ cup butter, softened
¼ cup cream cheese, softened
1 cup powdered monk fruit sweetener
¼ cup lemon juice

Directions
1. Preheat the oven to 350°F.
2. Line a loaf pan with parchment paper.
3. To make the cake, in a bowl, mix together the flour and baking powder.
4. In another bowl, add the eggs and monk fruit sweetener and blend with a hand mixer until slightly frothy.
5. Add the flour mixture, butter, lemon juice, and lemon extract and beat until well combined.
6. Place the dough in the prepared loaf pan.
7. Bake for about 45 minutes or until a toothpick inserted in the center comes out clean.
8. Remove the loaf pan from the oven and place on a wire rack for about 10 minutes.
9. Carefully invert the cake onto the wire rack to cool completely before frosting.
10. In a bowl, beat all of the frosting ingredients until smooth and creamy.
11. Spread the frosting evenly over the cake.
12. Slice and serve.

Nutrition (per serving)
Calories 371, fat 34.4 g, carbs 7.3 g, sugar 3.7 g,
Protein 3.7 g, sodium 176 mg

Tiramisu (Olive Garden)

A luscious and decadent Italian dessert for special occasions. This no-bake dessert is super easy to assemble but rich in taste.

Serves 2 | Prep time 15 minutes

Ingredients
Base
¼ cup almond flour
1–3 teaspoons powdered erythritol
Pinch of ground cinnamon
Pinch of salt
1½ teaspoons unsalted butter, melted
1 teaspoon strong brewed coffee

Tiramisu
2½ tablespoons heavy cream
⅓ cup mascarpone cheese, softened
2–3 tablespoons powdered erythritol
1 tablespoon dry white wine

Cocoa powder, for dusting

Directions
1. For the base, heat a dry skillet over medium heat and toast the almond flour for 2–4 minutes or until golden and fragrant, stirring continuously.
2. Remove from heat and transfer to a small bowl.
3. Add the erythritol, cinnamon, and salt and mix well.
4. Add the butter and coffee and mix well.
5. For the tiramisu, in a bowl, beat the heavy cream with an electric mixer until whipped.
6. Add the mascarpone cheese, erythritol, and wine and mix well.
7. Divide the base mixture into two serving glasses. Top with the cream mixture.
8. Refrigerate for at least 2 hours or up to overnight.
9. Dust with cocoa powder and serve.

Nutrition (per serving)
Calories 258, fat 22.7 g, carbs 4.6 g, sugar 0.7 g,
Protein 5.1 g, sodium 140 mg

Peach Cobbler (Cracker Barrel)

An old-fashioned peach cobbler recipe that is extremely easy to prepare. This recipe will surely become a family favorite.

Serves 8 | Prep time 15 minutes | Cooking time 45 minutes

Ingredients
Filling
1 pound peaches, peeled, cored, and sliced
2 tablespoons erythritol
¼ teaspoon xanthan gum

Topping
¾ cup almond flour
½ cup coconut flour
¼ cup erythritol
1½ teaspoons baking powder
¼ teaspoon salt

¾ cup heavy cream
¼ cup butter, melted
1 large egg, beaten, at room temperature
½ teaspoon ground cinnamon

Directions
1. Preheat the oven to 350°F. Arrange a rack in the center.
2. Grease a 9-inch pie plate.
3. For the filling, in a bowl, toss the peach slices with the erythritol and xanthan gum to coat well.
4. To make the topping, in another bowl, mix together the flours, erythritol, baking powder, and salt.
5. Add the heavy cream, butter, and beaten egg and mix until a thick mixture forms.
6. Arrange the peach slices at the bottom of the prepared pie plate. Top with the flour mixture.
7. Bake for 35–45 minutes. (You can cover with a piece of foil if the top becomes brown too quickly.)
8. Remove from the oven and sprinkle with cinnamon.
9. Set aside for 2–3 minutes before serving.

Nutrition (per serving)
Calories 208, fat 17 g, carbs 10.8 g, sugar 2.2 g,
Protein 2.3 g, sodium 133 mg

RECIPE INDEX

BREAKFAST RECIPES   21

Pink Drink (Starbucks)   29
Pumpkin Spice Frappuccino (Starbucks)   31
Ham and Cheese Omelet (Denny's)   33
Colorado Omelet (IHOP)   35
Cheese Omelet (Waffle House)   37
Egg Bites (Starbucks)   39
Breakfast Soufflé (Panera Bread)   41
Hash Brown Casserole (Cracker Barrel)   43
Chonaga Everything Bagel (Starbucks)   45
Waffles (Waffle House)   47
Wild Blueberry Muffins (Panera Bread)   49
Lemon Poppy Seed Bread (Starbucks)   51
Pumpkin Bread (Starbucks)   53
McGriddle Sandwich (McDonald's)   55

APPETIZER AND SNACK RECIPES   57

Artichoke-Spinach Dip (Olive Garden)   57
Queso Blanco (Applebee's)   59
Lettuce Wraps (PF Chang)   61
Bloomin' Onion (Outback Steakhouse)   63
Chicken Nuggets (Burger King)   65
Buffalo Wings (Cheesecake Factory)   67
Turkey Lettuce Wrap (Jimmy John's)   69
Green Beans Crisper (Applebee's)   71
Cheddar Bay Biscuit (Red Lobster)   73
Fried Mozzarella (Olive Garden)   75

SALAD AND SOUP RECIPES 77

Green Goddess Cobb Salad (Panera Bread) 77
Coleslaw (KFC) 79
Cucumber Tomato Salad (Cracker Barrel) 81
Salad (Olive Garden) 83
Cobb Salad (Cheesecake Factory) 85
Zuppa Toscana (Olive Garden) 87
Egg Drop Soup (Chinese Imperial Place) 89
Broccoli Cheddar Soup (Panera Bread) 91
Mushroom Truffle Bisque (Longhorn Steakhouse) 93
Tomato Basil Soup (Applebee) 95

CHICKEN RECIPES 97

Chicken Pot Pie (Cracker Barrel) 97
Chicken Marsala (Cheesecake Factory) 101
Chicken Madeira (Cheesecake Factory) 103
Chicken Limone (Buca de Beppo) 105
Chicken Picatta (Olive Garden) 107
Chicken Parmigiana (Olive Garden) 109
Mexican Grill Chicken (Chipotle) 111
Crispy Fried Chicken (KFC) 113
Instant Pot General Tso Chicken (Panda Express) 115
Chicken Tenders (Chick-fil-A) 117

BEEF AND PORK RECIPES 119

Chili (Wendy's) 119
Mongolian Beef (P.F. Chang) 121
Beef and Broccoli (P.F. Chang) 123
Beef Barbacoa (Chipotle) 125
Steak Fajita (Chili's) 127
Steak Diane (Cheesecake Factory) 129
Meatloaf (Cheesecake Factory) 131

Mexican Grill Pork Carnitas (Chipotle)   133
Grilled Pork Chop (Cheesecake Factory)   135
Baby Back Ribs (Outback Steakhouse)   137

FISH AND SEAFOOD RECIPES   139

Fresh Grilled Salmon (Cheesecake Factory)   139
Herb Crusted Salmon (Cheesecake Factory)   141
Pan-Fried Tilapia (Bonefish Grill)   143
Parmesan Crusted Tilapia (Olive Garden)   145
Tilapia Picatta (Olive Garden)   147
Shrimp Orleans (Chris Ruth Steakhouse)   149
Shrimp Scampi (Red Lobster)   151
Cajun Shrimp (Red Lobster)   153
Mussels di Napoli (Olive Garden)   155
Crab Cakes (Red Lobster)   157

DESSERT RECIPES   159

Chocolate Frosty (Wendy's)   159
Zabaglione (Olive Garden)   161
Glazed Doughnuts (Krispy Kreme)   163
Cranberry Bliss Bars (Starbucks)   165
Original Cheesecake (Cheesecake Factory)   167
Pumpkin Cheesecake (Cheesecake Factory)   169
Lemon Pound Cake (Starbucks)   171
Tiramisu (Olive Garden)   173
Peach Cobbler (Cracker Barrel)   175

APPENDIX

Cooking Conversion Charts

1. Measuring Equivalent Chart

Type	Imperial	Imperial	Metric
Weight	1 dry ounce		28 g
	1 pound	16 dry ounces	0.45 kg
Volume	1 teaspoon		5 ml
	1 dessert spoon	2 teaspoons	10 ml
	1 tablespoon	3 teaspoons	15 ml
	1 Australian tablespoon	4 teaspoons	20 ml
	1 fluid ounce	2 tablespoons	30 ml
	1 cup	16 tablespoons	240 ml
	1 cup	8 fluid ounces	240 ml
	1 pint	2 cups	470 ml
	1 quart	2 pints	0.95 l
	1 gallon	4 quarts	3.8 l
Length	1 inch		2.54 cm

* Numbers are rounded to the closest equivalent

2. Oven Temperature Equivalent Chart

Fahrenheit (°F)	Celsius (°C)	Gas Mark
220	100	
225	110	1/4
250	120	1/2
275	140	1
300	150	2
325	160	3
350	180	4
375	190	5
400	200	6
425	220	7
450	230	8
475	250	9
500	260	

* Celsius (°C) = T (°F)-32] * 5/9
** Fahrenheit (°F) = T (°C) * 9/5 + 32
*** Numbers are rounded to the closest equivalent

Made in United States
Orlando, FL
29 June 2023